We cannot know how much we learn
From those who never will return,
Until a flash of unforeseen
Remembrance falls on what has been.

Edward Arlington Robinson

# Write & Publish Your Life Story: Guaranteed!

## by BetteLou Tobin

Windstorm Creative Limited
Port Orchard, Washington

Write & Publish Your Life Story: Guaranteed!
copyright 1999 by BetteLou Tobin
published by Windstorm Creative

ISBN 1-886383-61-8

9 8 7 6 5 4
Third revised edition 2/2001.

Cover by Buster Blue of Blue Artisans.
Interior design by Windstorm Creative.

Windstorm Creative is a six imprint, international organization involved in publishing books in all genres including electronic publications; producing games, toys, videos and audio cassettes as well as producing theatre, film and visual arts events.

Windstorm Creative Ltd.
7419 Ebbert Drive Southeast
Port Orchard WA 98367
360-769-7174
autobio@windstormcreative.com
www.windstormcreative.com

# Write & Publish Your Life Story: Guaranteed!

## by BetteLou Tobin

Windstorm Creative Limited
Port Orchard, Washington

# Dedication

To my husband
Rick Tobin
in loving memory

# Acknowledgments

Carter Tobin
Corielle Tobin
John Frazzini
Michael Karash
Jennifer DiMarco

# Contents

## PART I:  Writing Skills and Guidance

## PART II:  Self Interviewing Questions

# PART III: Setting Up

# PART IV: Afterword

## AN IMPORTANT NOTE FROM THE PUBLISHER

As you are reading Ms. Tobin's book please keep in mind that there are many approaches to writing. Ms. Tobin offers a textbook-perfect approach — meaning that she tells you how to write your book while observing the rules of grammar, punctuation, etc. This is a very appealing format to most writers because it assures — through the clear, uniform format — that their ideas will be easily understood. However, you may want to write your life story using your own lexicon. You may wish to write your story as you speak — after all, very few of us speak with perfect grammar or 100% correct phrasing. You may even want to write your life story as one long poem! This books is one way. But not the only way. As long as you read and follow the directions in Part IV, your book will be published — no matter what approach you choose.

# PART I

## Introduction from BetteLou

## Writing Skills and Guidance

You have been wanting to write your life story, but you just haven't been able to get started, right? This book will get you started, guide you along the way and show you how to set it up. The first part offers some hints and writing skills. The second part has self interviewing questions to jog your memory. The third part is for use when you finish writing.

Before you get to the self interviewing questions, bone up on some of the mechanics to give you competence and a little incentive. Perhaps you only want to write about a certain period in your life. Go for it, you might have a great novel. You should still complete the book so you will leave a total record of yourself and your lifestyle. Refer back to the writing skills as needed, but don't be put off by inhibitions about writing techniques or spelling. Just get busy and enjoy being an author. Start a precedent of writing your autobiography and your family and friends will want to do the same.

Of course, not every question will pertain to your individual experiences and you don't have to answer all the ones that do. As you read through the different phases and particulars that chronicle your history, you will be reminded of stories connected with certain events. These stories and facts are going to become a comprehensive and detailed autobiography that will be a cherished gift to your descendants. I will be right there offering help and encouragement.

Load up on note pads and pens or pencils. You might want to use a tape recorder. It is essential to make written or verbal notes as soon as possible after an incident comes to mind. If you don't jot it down, you will forget it.

If you are a ghost writer for a friend or relative who is unable to do the actual writing because of poor eyesight or a physical challenge, read the book aloud and ask the questions, taking notes or using a tape recorder.

Turn your notes into a series of stories. Try to be honest, direct, fair, specific and interesting. Be a name dropper. Mention as many people and places as you can. Try to be accurate because you might be telling tales about a reader's great grand parent. Don't be afraid to jump right in. Writing is a passion. It is also a chore. This project should become so important to you that everything else will have to fit into your writing schedule. You can do it. Recording an experience will bring back feelings and emotions, a smile, a laugh. Sometimes your eyes may fill with tears. The book is going to be a labor of love.

Each morning, while you are having breakfast, assemble your notes. Make a habit of carrying your note pads with you everywhere. Don't underestimate points of interest. So many things that were commonplace years ago are obsolete now. People enjoy hearing and reading about the past. Be truthful and authentic, although you can certainly exaggerate a bit and call it poetic license. If, however, you are inclined to tell tall tales, try to keep a tight rein on yourself. Remember, this is supposed to be a factual account of your life. Save the fiction for your next book. I don't mean that it has to be dry and boring. Put lots of humor and other emotions down as they come to you, have fun.

Gather old photographs and mementos. Have them on hand to help you recall people and places. Get in touch with friends and relatives to share in your endeavors. Throw a special party. Go over letters, scrap books, year books and pictures together. Ask everyone to write something about you or your family history to include in your book. When you see how much you can come up with, you will know you are well on your way to a complete autobiography.

This is just the beginning. A lot of your memories deal with your childhood, but we are not going to dwell exclusively on your young life. I have a wide range of topics for you to cover. Some recollections will be difficult to write. Get through them as best you can. If you feel some areas are too sensitive or too painful, go on to another category and write about something pleasant. Unhappy memories will probably be easier to document later as you gain confidence in your writing ability. Sometimes the difficult passages are necessary in order to fill in gaps or to round out the whole picture.

Even if you don't have direct descendants, you can write your autobiography. You are making a statement verifying your existence. You certainly have a lot of friends and relatives who want to read all about your life. Go through the writing skills and questions, just ignore all the references to children and grandchildren. You are a unique individual. You have stories to tell about your presence on this earth and your influence on people and the environment. Whoever you are, relate the essence of your being.

## MOTIVATION

Why write your autobiography? If you need motives, here are some. You are writing in order to:

1) Tell your story.

2)  Narrate events of the past.

3)  Show how your character was shaped.

4)  Gather information on family history.

5)  Pay tribute where it is due.

6)  Bear witness - observe.

7)  Chronicle times.

8)  Set the record straight.

9)  Get it down before it is lost.

10) Clarify or expose issues.

11) Expose wrongdoing.

12) Champion a cause.

13) Give advice or guidelines.

14) Sound a warning.

15) Share the hard times and the glory.

16) Come to terms with the past.

17) Make some confessions.

18) Inspire and encourage future generations.

19) Present your theories and philosophies.

20) Merely entertain.

21) Immortalize personalities in your life.

22) Immortalize yourself.

Add whatever reasons or motives you like. This will be more than something to simply pass the time. It is going to be a real challenge. Lots of people have done it. You will work hard and you will love it.

# RESEARCH

If you feel the need to clarify dates, names or facts, do some research. There are many sources to turn to for help. Start with your public library. Ask for assistance in finding genealogical and historical records. Librarians can help you to access census records also. The federal census began in 1790 and has been taken every 10 years since then. Because of the privacy act, information can only be obtained from 70 years ago. During the '90's you can check up to 1920. By the year 2000, you will be able to get 1930 records. You might delve into courthouse archives, old newspapers or church registers. Adoption records can be opened in many cases. You will have to consult your state policy on adoption records.

You can retrieve military information from:

MILITARY SERVICE RECORDS
(NNCC)
National Archives (GSA)
Washington,DC 20408

Ask for war pension records also. You can write for these three pamphlets that cover all states.

BIRTH AND DEATH RECORDS
Public Health Publications #630A

MARRIAGE RECORDS
Public Health Publications #630B

DIVORCE RECORDS
Public Health Publications #630C
There is a nominal fee. Contact:
Superintendent of Documents

United States Government Printing Office
Washington, DC 20402

With some recollections you might want to show comparisons to current statistics, i.e., population then and now, climate, pollution, crime, etc. Contact your chamber of commerce or a television weather station for some useful information.

For some reasons you may want to go to state, city or county clerks for property or asset searches. Employment, social security, academic profiles, tax, credit, bankruptcies, liens, judgments, criminal searches will probably have to be conducted by a licensed person. If you hire a private investigator, make sure he or she is reputable and the prices are reasonable. You might call Extreme Internet to find what databases are available for lists of public records.

Fill out the family tree chart and make some charts for other members of your family with their lines of heritage. Don't simply record statistics, flesh out the stories with descriptions, feelings, attitudes, impressions, frustrations, changes. You know what they say in the theatre, "You can be anything but boring."

## PHOTOGRAPHS

Make sure you have plenty of good photos to sprinkle throughout the book. Caption each picture as best you can, who is in the picture, when and where it was taken, your age at the time. A good way to get started on a subject is to look through old photos while you are reading the questions. Go to a copy shop to have copies made of your photographs. The newer copy machines can reproduce your photos nicely in color or black and white. If you plan to revisit some of the people and places in your past, don't forget to bring your camera. Put some "then and now" comparisons in your pages. Ask to borrow photos of people and places that might help, make copies and return them.

If you don't have a recent photo of yourself, have some taken. Get out the camera and take shots of trophies, keepsakes, documents, some of your favorite ornaments, paintings, furniture, hobbies, pets, current friends and relatives. When you paste pictures on pages, use a rubberized glue. It is less likely to wrinkle the paper. You are just getting started. Don't stop with this bit of nostalgia, get on to the writing. You should have a big, thick book.

## GETTING STARTED

You don't have to start your book with the order in which I have set up the questions. Begin with your life as it is now, if you like, and then go through the rest in a series of flashbacks. A good way to open is to relate one particular memorable event or turning point in your life. This could be something that had an impact on your life either as a child or as an adult. Get the readers' attention with an interesting story and they will want to read more about you. Then you can fill in with your youth and follow the guidelines so your book will have form and substance.

This first story can be about a horrendous accident that altered your lifestyle. It might be a certain trip, a beginning or ending, a special gift, meeting a wonderful person, or the loss of someone close to you. It may be a tale you have told many times or it may be bottled up inside you and needs telling.

You might want to begin with a history of your ancestors or how you, your parents or grandparents came to America. This first story can be a short paragraph or several pages long. When you gather information and start going through the questions, you will need direction. Use these key words to help focus on your memories.

WHO?—Name the characters involved.

WHAT?—What was the event, what happened?

WHERE?—Give the place of occurrence.

WHEN?—Put down the date and time.

WHY?—List the significance or reasons.

HOW?—Tell the circumstances leading up to it.

Keep these questions in mind while you make notes. What was your age at the time? If you don't remember the exact date, just tell the season, the time of day, the weather. How were you connected to the events? What were the consequences?

Putting the first words down can be simply setting the mood or climate. Use descriptive phrases to set up the story, such as; "It was hot." Then explain just how the heat affected you. Use your sense memory to take your readers to that time and place.

"We were having fun." All right, remember the key words, who, what, where, when, why, and how. Who else was involved? Approximately how old were you? Where were you? Why were you there? What happened next?

"I was scared." Everyone has felt fear, perhaps not with the intensity of your experience, share your feelings. Was this a recent fright or did it happen when you were a child? Take us there. Were the people around you scared also? How long did it last?

Try out some intriguing opening lines to suit you.

"She was beautiful."

"I didn't see it coming."

"The icy wind was paralyzing."

"Are you ready for this?"

"I was so proud."

"I was born in a trunk."

Think of a catchy phrase to start and just let it flow.   What emotions were displayed?   Was it a conflict, a funny anecdote or a serious confrontation? What was the high point, humorous, scary, dangerous or tragic?

Write as though you are telling the story to someone.   It may come to you in bits and pieces. You will remember tidbits, maybe just images of people or incidents of an important event.   You may think it is not interesting enough to record.   You were there.   Not every recollection has to be a story with a beginning, a middle and an end.   If you have a fond memory of something, there is a reason, share it.

You might like to choose a subtitle for your autobiography based on your opening story and this would explain the title right away.   Or you can name the book after something significant, such as a nickname and how you acquired it.   Pick a symbol of some sort, a place, a season, a hobby or skill, a profession.   You might even use a line of a poem or song or a favorite expression.   Of course you don't have to have a subtitle, it's only a suggestion.

## CONVERSATIONAL SPEECH

Try to write using the same vernacular that you use in casual conversation. It will be easier for you to express yourself. Your speech patterns will allow the flavor of your personality to show through, however, you should have some guidelines to make your work palatable. Aim for clarity so that your readers will not have to struggle to interpret your meaning. If you are not sure of the definition or spelling of a word, look it up. Make use of a dictionary and a thesaurus. Use tact and good sense. Balance explanations with clearly understood terminology to avoid confusion. Employ quotation marks, parentheses, dashes or commas if need be to define words or statements.

EXAMPLES:
1) Appropriate words, "politically correct," should be used in order to not offend anyone.
2) Passive restraints, (air bags) may add hundreds of dollars to the price of cars.
3) Plea bargaining — which is the practice of pleading guilty to a less serious offense instead of being tried for a more serious one — is increasing in our overburdened courts.
4) The use of dialogue, the lines your characters speak, will enhance your narrative technique.

Explain or define technological terminology which may only be understood in the context of certain professions, such as; computers, medicine, photography, plumbing, electronics, etc.

Avoid vagueness, words which do not convey a precise meaning or description, such as; "It was okay." "There was a lot of stuff." "We lived in a house."

Try not to repeat words or phrases for lack of more interesting vocabulary, such as; "It was a nice day, the people were nice and we had a nice time." Read over your work and if you notice that you are starting too many sentences with the same word, choose other words or change the structure of the sentence. You don't want the first words of every sentence in a paragraph to read, "I said," "I went," "I saw," "I had."

Diction is the choice of words. Formal diction is used in scientific or legal papers. Informal diction is popular usage which is easy to understand. Colloquial diction is regional dialect or expression. It's okay to use colloquialisms if they fit in your speech patterns, They are often unique and can add colorful idioms to your autobiography. Observe and record accents and dialects of family and friends, as well as your own. This is part of your history, but be aware of sounding trite by too much usage of cliché expressions. Some figures of speech and repetitions can wear thin. Try to avoid using phrases too often such as; "like," "you know," "you see," "like I said," "but um," "so, anyway," "I go," "I says." Certain slang words are more annoying than cute.

A recent slang phenomenon is the use or misuse of the word "at." You will hear "at" tacked on to the ends of questions such as, "When is it?" "Where do you live?" "Where do you want it?" It doesn't belong there. Curtail the use of curse words, they are an excuse for thinking.

After awhile you will get used to monitoring yourself for common mistakes. If grammar is going to be a worry, have someone proofread your papers or maybe bone up on some basics yourself. The best thing is to go along with my instructions and let it all hang out. The objective here after all is what you have to say.  This is your book, go for it.

## CHARACTER SKETCHES

Think of this chapter as an assignment.  You have to write a character sketch by next Tuesday.  There must be at least one person who stands out in your memory as an influential character.  You may just want to tell about someone whom you admired.  Your choice may be a relative or close friend who figured in more than one memorable event in your life.  Write a character study and then when you mention this individual as you go through various interview topics, your readers will already know and feel his or her presence.  This is a great way to bring back memories.  Once you begin, you will want to detail more people who made an impression on you.

You will have a great deal to draw from if you write about a friend or spouse with whom you spent a lot of time.  How has this person changed over the years?  Include some dialogue to show his or her manner of speaking.  It breaks up the narrative and makes the person more familiar.

Everyone has a story about a teacher or clergyman, a neighbor, friend or coworker.  What was your first impression?  It is not always necessary to delve into his or her background unless certain facts are relevant to an anecdote.  In some cases recounting past events that shaped the life of your subject will help to understand idiosyncrasies.  Be selective, just don't clutter your paper with boring details.

If you write about someone whom you met briefly, state the approximate date and time in your life.  What impact did this person have on you?  You may opt to write about a political figure, a famous artist, an actor, a scientist.  This can be a person you knew or someone who lived long ago.   State the reasons for your choices.

When you have your subject in mind, begin with a dominate personality trait.  Try to give an example of it by relating actions or speech.  This will serve to introduce your character's personality and to spark interest in the readers.  Think of several adjectives that would fit the qualities you noticed.  Would you say he/she was kind, generous, stubborn, compassionate, comical?  What effect did this person have on you and others?  What was the energy level?  Describe the physical being by using similes or metaphors.   Was there an outstanding feature?  Describe facial expressions, attitude, movement.  What reaction did people have to his or her presence, respect, awe, humor, fear, comfort, love?  How were you treated?

Very often the manner of dress gives clues to a personality.  You may remember this person wearing rumpled, ill fitting clothes or out of date fashions.  Maybe the clothes were stylish, casual or elegant.  Perhaps they were patched yet clean, or expensive yet poor taste.

If you can, write a story about this character, how obstacles were overcome, problems solved.  You don't have to tell a definite story, this is an exercise in character study.   Bring your essay to a conclusion.  Did your first impression change?  Use the traits that stand out to end the sketch.   For instance;   "Despite his cockeyed optimism, he worried about..."   "Yes, he would give you the shirt off his back, providing he had another one."   "I am sure that where ever she is, there are freshly baked cookies available."   "His contribution to the world of science is immeasurable."

Do this one for now.  It should be at least one full page.  How nice it would be for you to write a series of testimonials depicting the people who have touched your life.

## DIALOGUE

Unless you have total recall, you will not remember exact dialogue. Use dialogue anyway to add spice to your narrative. You know the gist of certain conversations, so take poetic license. Some stories really call for direct dialogue to get the essence of confrontations or intimacies. Use it sparingly if it seems stilted and unnatural. If you find writing dialogue too difficult, go to a library and look up some short stories by Theodore Dreiser. His technique is very effective. You should read autobiographies of other people, although some people feel that reading about the lives of famous personages is rather intimidating. Don't be put off writing about yourself. What you have to offer is unique.

### DIRECT DIALOGUE
Use quotation marks for direct quotes set off by commas.
EXAMPLES: Sam asked, "Are you going to march in the parade?"
"If our costumes arrive on time we will," I said.

### INDIRECT DIALOGUE
EXAMPLES: Sam asked if we were going to march in the parade. I assured him we would if our costumes arrived on time.

DIRECT EXAMPLES: John asked, "Will you carry a rose so I can spot you?"
"I shall wear a bright red rose in my hair," Nell replied.

INDIRECT EXAMPLES: John asked Nell to carry a rose so he could spot her. She told him she would wear a bright red rose in her hair.

SPEAKER TAGS
(Words that identify the speaker)
EXAMPLES: "Where have you been?" Helen demanded. "Mom," Sue said, "I went shopping."

SPEAKER UNIDENTIFIED
EXAMPLES: "And just where have you been, young lady?"
"I told you I was going shopping, Mom."
In this case the speaker is recognized by inference and a tag is not necessary. This method is especially useful for a rapid or heated exchange of words. Just don't make it confusing as to who is saying what to whom. Try a variety of tags to break the monotony of -he said-she said.

EXAMPLES: Joe staggered in, moaning, "I am dead tired." Her voice shrill with excitement, "Go, Danny! Run!" Startled, I blurted out, "Where did you come from?"

Play with different ways of setting up dialogue. It's not difficult and it will become easier as you continue.

## ACCURACY OF INFORMATION

In your autobiography you will be commenting on past or current events, family history, news, political figures and more. Perhaps you will be giving instructions or hints for a hobby or interest. You should clarify the information given as to probable or accurate facts. Be aware of your choice of words. If your purpose is just to make generalized observations or arguments about something, use words such as; might have, maybe, possibly, could be, supposedly, probably, appear to be, seeming, in all likelihood. These words reflect a probable cause or conclusion. You may also make an educated guess. It is called an induction.

INDUCTIVE REASONING
This begins with an observation, an example or a guess not backed by scientific evidence.

EXAMPLES: "I bought this book because I liked another book by the same author." "It seems To be a good place to eat, judging by the many cars in the parking lot." "Children whose parents smoke are likely to pick up the nasty habit also." "His ankles are quite swollen, possibly due to congestive heart failure." "Apparently, the murder weapon was thrown away."

You don't have to be an absolute stickler on the logic of every subject. You know that fire burns, so you do not have to touch the fire to come to the conclusion that it is true. When you are giving information that involves reasoning, the accuracy of your conclusion is determined by your purpose.

EXAMPLES: "Supermarket brand items are cheaper than other commercial brand items." "The monsoons hit Arizona in August." "Seatbelts save lives."

Are these statements educated guesses or casual observances or are they reliable based on proven facts? If they are proven facts, they are called deductions.

DEDUCTIVE REASONING

This backs up the conclusion of a matter with scientific evidence.  When you are sure of your facts and can support them with reliable sources, you can be more definite with your pronouncements. Remember that your premise should be logically sound and previously determined to be truthful and correct.

EXAMPLE:  "Surplus energy from too much fatty or sugary food is stored in the body as fat and can become a serious health problem."

Sometimes facts and figures given out by companies, politicians or authorities become distorted.  Certain groups with self interests or monetary gains tend to be biased.

EXAMPLE: "The tobacco industry gave strong arguments against the theory that cigarette smoking causes cancer."

The truth may be obscured by using persuasive advertising or clouding the issue.  Use your good judgment.  Check your sources to assure that your information is accurate if you wish to make deductive statements. 'Nuff said.

## TRANSITIONS

Transitions are words or phrases denoting a change in time, place, mood or action.  They are used to explain or set up parts of your story without going into a lot of particulars.

EXAMPLES:
1) Exhausted, Jill fell into a deep sleep.  Bright

morning sunlight streaming through her window forced her eyes open. "Nine o'clock! Oh my God." She started another busy day at a dead run. This transition implies that Jill overslept and that she would be late.

2) Bill checked into the hotel at 3pm wearing a worn business suit. By 6pm he was decked out in a tuxedo with a wine colored cummerbund and bow tie to match. He was ready. There was no need to describe Bill unpacking, showering, shaving and dressing, unless it had some relevance to the plot.

3) Jean was enjoying the evening out with her friends. The conversation at the table was stimulating. The cozy ambiance, excellent food and charming companions lifted her spirits. She laughed, Made a witty remark and the next voice she heard was that of a paramedic hovering over her in an ambulance. She'd had a seizure. Perhaps a detailed description of her seizures had been written before or will be explained later.

Be careful how you use transitions. Keep the thread of your story clear. This is an interesting way to project your characters into another time frame or situation without becoming boring.

## POWER WORDS

Starting a sentence with a power word or phrase gets the readers' attention and sparks interest.

EXAMPLES:   "Explosive temper tantrums jeopardized his position on the team."   "Withering looks from Sister Clair kept us in line."   "Dancing was Amy's passion every waking moment."   Those examples are a bit more exciting than the following.

EXAMPLES:   "His position on the team was jeopardized by his temper tantrums."   "We were kept in line by the withering looks from Sister Clair." "Every waking moment Amy's passion was dancing."

Ending a sentence with a strong word or phrase is an effective way to prove a point or to punch up an idea.

EXAMPLES:   "Cigarette smoking contributes to the development of many ailments, but for lung and heart diseases, it is the leading cause of death." "Little did Tom know that his joke would end in tragedy."   "The Governor realized he was not above the law when he was indicted for twenty two counts of fraud."   Play with these choices for emphasis, but don't get so hung up on word placement that you interrupt the flow of thought.   The next Example gives information, however, it would make much better copy if the power words are restructured either at the beginning or the end of the sentence.

EXAMPLE: "After the hurricane, the residents were met with total devastation when they returned to their homes." (Beginning - catch the readers' interest)   "Total devastation awaited the residents returning to their homes after the hurricane."   (Ending - punch it up)   "Returning to their homes after the hurricane, residents were met with total devastation."

Read over your work and alter word placement

or add power words for effect if you like. It will add another dimension to your artistry.

Another reason for editing your work is to watch for bureaucratese. This is the practice of using big words and phrases to put across an idea instead of simple, more appropriate words. Government writing is especially guilty of using official sounding but confusing language.

EXAMPLE: "The maximum potential of this prototype depends upon an extended scenario of the financial configuration of the future earnings after costs and the feasibility of manufacturing, precluding the advisability of the majority of management to subsequently ratify a commitment." I don't even know what I said here. You get the picture, so if you are used to writing this type of language in your business, please don't use it for your autobiography. Of course you can use big or small words, long or short sentences to convey your meaning. Just be cautious of the B word.

## SUSPENSE

If you have a story with a mystery, don't give it away in the beginning. Play with it. Build suspense, you know the ending. Start with a conflict, perhaps a philosophical struggle between people or within yourself. It could be over moral values, greed, political issues, jealousy, whatever it is that needs to be resolved. Plan your story with a surprise ending in mind. How were your characters involved? What obstacles had to be overcome? Was there a murder? a disappearance? a strange occurrence? If it is a humorous anecdote, go for the laughs. Make it campy or wild. If it is scary, keep us on the edge of our seats. Make us cry over the sad parts and wonder at the unexplained mysteries. Were you there as an observer, a victim or a winner? Give hints throughout the story that show the ending could go either way.

Remember to focus on the story line and not go off on tangents unless they are relevant to the point you are making. Set up your scenes and characters with some colorful descriptive phrases. Then forget about dressing up every sentence. When you are conveying a fast paced action story, you don't want to lose your momentum. Keep up the interest, make it sound probable. Read through the categories and when you are reminded of an incident with any kind of mystery surrounding it, tell it with action. Create suspense, rewrite and edit until you are satisfied with the results.

## DESCRIPTIVE WORDS AND PHRASES

Colorful words are inviting. You can create beauty, intrigue, fear, suspense, humor, all with your choices of adjectives. Some people pepper their conversations with expressive idioms that depict verbal pictures, but most people find it hard to come up with specific adjectives to describe something. Please don't sit for hours trying to think of just the right word when you have a story to tell. If it will help, make lists of descriptive words and phrases that might dress up your work. Use them as you write, so you won't become discouraged waiting for a specific word to pop into your head.

Use the proper names of things if you like, but for variety and interest try to be a little creative. Here are some examples. "The Cirrus Uncinus clouds are delicate white filaments, also known as horses' tails. Altocumulus Perlucidus clouds are called buttermilk skies. Nimbostratus clouds, low, ragged, dark clouds, heavy with snow or rain." Use your imagination. Think up some delightful or moody descriptions to suit your purpose.

CLOUDS: cotton candy, puffy shapes of poodles and bunnies, ominous, foreboding or grim thunder clouds, fluorescent salmon pink, dark clouds with silver linings.

PERSONALITIES: lovable old curmudgeon, cantankerous old fool, irascible old fogy, gruff demeanor with a big heart, charming gentleman, sparkling wit, gallant, serious, studious, sweet, coy, precious, loving, caring, tender, understanding, giving, kind, darling, happy-go-lucky.

FEATURES: Eyes; deep-set, magnetic, fiery, blazing, bulging, smiling, sky-blue, sad, twinkling, piercing. Noses; aquiline, Roman, pert, button, tilted, broken. Faces; rosy glow, sallow complexion, haggard look, bloom of youth, weak chin, receding hairline, scrawny neck, strong jaw, pinched, care-worn, pallor of death, chubby cheeks.

ANGER; boiling mad, seething animosity, cold fury, resentful, hot under the collar, flushed with rage, madder than a wet hen, blew his top, held a grudge, lost control.

WEATHER: stifling humidity, shroud-like mist, bone-chilling fog, rain pelted forest, crisp autumn day, scorching heat, smell of spring, warm lazy day, bitter cold, perfect snow conditions for skiing.

SOUND: thunderous crash, ear-splitting shriek, deafening roar, rustling leaves, incessant ringing, tinkling bells, blaring music, cackling laughter, bellowing, ranting, screaming, whispering, banging, thumping, melodic, cacophonous din.

You get the idea.   You may notice that you have used the same description three times in one paragraph.   Change it with synonyms.   Keep a thesaurus handy to extend your vocabulary.   Be inventive, but don't go crazy.   Fill in important facts, adjust sequences if need be, add a character you forgot and stuff in some adjectives.

## COMPARISONS

Figures of speech are used by writers to add depth and color to their work.   You have heard and spoken comparisons in figures of speech all your life. Here is a little technical information you might find useful.

SIMILE:   A simile compares things using the words - like, as or so.   In some ways "A" is like "B." Feelings or qualities are associated with one to the other.

EXAMPLE:   "Good as gold,"   "Cute as a button,"   "Like thy rocks of towering grandeur, make me strong and sure,"   "Smooth words like gold enameled fish,"   "And honeyed words like bees, gilded and sticky, with a little sting"

METAPHOR:   A metaphor compares things by identifying one with the other.   "A" is "B."   The description of a subject is enlivened by imagery.

EXAMPLE:   "He is a rock,"   "She is putty in his hands,"   "But at my back I always hear Time's winged chariot hurrying near,"   "The fog comes on little cat feet," "Warm, lazy words, white cattle under trees," He has muscles of steel," She has eagle eyes," "Mouth of a river," "Face of a clock"

Adjectives have three degrees of comparison; The POSITIVE, the COMPARATIVE, the SUPERLATIVE.

1. The POSITIVE degree is used when the adjective modifies a noun or pronoun without comparing it to another of the same thing. It names the simple quality.

   EXAMPLE: "Bill is a strong man," "Her eyes are as blue as a summer sky." "Usually the words [as——as] are used in this degree when comparing one thing to something else.

2. The COMPARATIVE degree is used when comparing two things with different qualities of the same trait. It expresses a higher degree of the quality.

   EXAMPLE: "Bill is stronger than Bob," John is taller than I" The words} [than I am tall] are either used or implied. "John is taller than me," is wrong, but that is another lesson about pronoun agreement.

   EXAMPLE: "Pat is older than she" The words [than she is old] is implied. "Pat is older than her," is wrong. You may use some raunchy expressions in your own speech , such as; "It was colder than a well digger's a—." Go ahead and use those sayings if they are part of your lingo, after all, this is not a formal document, it is your life, warts and all.

   Many adjectives of one syllable simply add -r- or -er- to form the COMPARATIVE degree, i.e. larger, smaller, higher, kinder, finer, etc.

EXAMPLE: "The corn is sweeter this year." The understanding, "than it was last year," is implied.

The word -more- often precedes adjectives of two or more syllables when used in the COMPARATIVE degree.

EXAMPLE: "Sue is more practical than I am." "The maneuvers get more complicated." "Driving is more dangerous in the rain."

Remember to leave the adjective itself alone when you add - more- so you won't get phrases like, "more faster," "more prettier," "more stupider."

3. The SUPERLATIVE degree is used in comparing three or more persons or things. Almost all adjectives of one syllable form the SUPERLATIVE by adding -st- or -est- "cutest, loudest, fastest."

EXAMPLES: "Of all the girls, Carol had the nicest smile." "The tallest building in town." "He was the bravest man."
Most adjectives of two or more syllables use -most- before the simple adjective in the SUPERLATIVE form.

EXAMPLES: "He was the most considerate man I knew." "Sally had the most fascinating doll collection." "Peter was the most active baby." "She has the most beautiful garden."

The same with -most-, leave the adjective alone when you use -most-, so you won't say, "She had the most recenter file." "He was the most carefuler camper."

IRREGULAR FORMS: This term applies to words that change to form their own degrees of comparisons.

| POSITIVE | COMPARATIVE | SUPERLATIVE |
|----------|-------------|-------------|
| bad/ill | worse | worst |
| good/well | better | best |
| many/much | more | most |
| up | upper | uppermost |

Some irregular adjectives and adverbs change forms according to meaning or intent.

little      littler (in size)      littlest (in size)
less (in amount)      least (in amount)

far      farther (distance)      farthest (distance)
further (degree)      furthest (degree)

There are some adjectives that do not theoretically compare in degrees. Dead does not get deader even though you have heard the expression, "Deader than a doornail." Empty means just that, how can it be emptier or more empty? Square, circular, perfect, single, unique, complete, perpetual, these are some absolutes that stand on their own. You don't need to add superlatives like more perfect or very unique.

I don't want to confuse you with English lessons. You may not need instructions in this area; however, it doesn't hurt to brush up on your writing skills now and then. For some people, learning the "whys and wherefores" of a subject will aid in the practical usage of it.

What are adjectives anyway? What does modifying mean? An adjective is a describing word. It gives a quality or quantity of a noun or pronoun.

To modify means to specify, qualify or limit; "red dress," "funny face," "closest relative." Nouns and pronouns can even be used as adjectives; "Jim's shirt," "body lotion," "her nails," "my book." Numerals are used as adjectives also; "second string," "nine players," etc.

An INFINITIVE PHRASE may function as an adjective. The infinitive is a verbal noun usually introduced by the word -to-. It must be logically related to the word it modifies.

EXAMPLES: "I frequent malls to shop and bookstores to browse." "She has sweaters to be cleaned."

Be careful of misplaced modifiers.

EXAMPLES: "To wake up on time, the alarm must be set." WRONG! The alarm doesn't wake up. "To wake up on time, you must set the alarm." RIGHT!
"I asked her the next time to bake my favorite pie." WRONG! "I asked her to bake my favorite pie the next time." RIGHT!

A PREPOSITIONAL PHRASE used as an adjective usually is placed after the noun it modifies.

EXAMPLES: "This is not the place for this discussion." "He sent a book of love poems."
A preposition must have an object.

A PARTICIPIAL PHRASE starts with the stem of a verb, but is used as an adjective. It names an action that the noun does or has done to it.

EXAMPLES: "Having skated in the Nationals,

Jim tried for the Olympics." "The actors, having been well rehearsed, gave a fine performance."

I'm sure you have heard of the dreaded dangling participle. The dangle happens if the participle is not attached to a noun able to do the action it names or to have the action done to it.

EXAMPLES: "Rowing across the lake, the dock was reached in a half hour." WRONG! The dock can't row. "Rowing across the lake, we reached the dock in a half hour." RIGHT! - we can row.
"While dawdling in the museum, the bus was missed." WRONG! The bus didn't dawdle. "While dawdling in the museum, we missed the bus." RIGHT! But next time, don't dawdle.

Adjectives modify nouns or pronouns. Adverbs modify other parts of sentences, verbs, adjectives or other adverbs. Adverbs tell how, when or where. Sometimes they end in -ly-. The same words can be used as adjectives or adverbs depending upon their function in the sentences.

EXAMPLES: "The rotten egg smells bad." The adjective -bad- modifies egg. "The rotten egg smells badly," would imply that the egg has the ability to use a nose. This is the misuse of an adverb. "Gus feels bad." "Gus feels badly." The first sentence says that Gus is ill or unhappy. Bad is an adjective modifying the noun Gus. The second sentence says that Gus has an impaired sense of touch. Badly is an adverb modifying the verb feels. So, adverbs suggest the manner in which the verbs are used.

MISPLACED MODIFIERS; Be careful how and where you place adjectives and adverbs to avoid confusion.

EXAMPLES: "I only repeated the gossip about the trade to Joe." What does this mean? I and nobody else repeated the gossip to Joe? If so, then change the sentence to show that only acts as an adjective modifying the pronoun I. "Only I repeated the gossip about the trade to Joe." Does it mean, I repeated the gossip and nothing else to Joe? If so, change it to, "I repeated to Joe, only the gossip about the trade." Only is the adjective modifying the noun clause, the gossip about the trade. Does it mean, I told Joe and no one else? If so, only is an adverb modifying the verb repeated. "I repeated only to Joe the gossip about the trade." Try to place the modifier near the word you want to modify.

All of this may be of no consequence, however, if while you are writing something that doesn't seem quite right, don't call me, instead dig around in these pages for a solution, or sound out the problem to someone and straighten it out. Let's put them all together.

SIMILE = She runs like a deer.

METAPHOR = She is a gazelle.

POSITIVE DEGREE = She runs as graceful as a deer.

COMPARATIVE DEGREE = She runs faster than I.

SUPERLATIVE DEGREE = She is the fastest runner on the team.

INFINITIVE PHR. = To run fast, she must stay in shape.

PREPOSITIONAL PHR. = She wins races for the glory.

PARTICIPIAL PHR. = Having trained hard, she won easily.

Clear as a bell? Try mixing them up and see how you do. Oh, the heck with it, go on with your writing! —Go on!

## GRAMMAR

One of the reasons given for putting off writing an autobiography is the confusion about grammar. This chapter gives some grammatical tips and cites some common errors. If you really want to polish your skills, you can get help from English textbooks in libraries or you may take a course at a community college. You might just go to it and have someone else correct and shape your manuscript. The important thing is to get it done. Even if you feel that grammar is not a problem, you should skim through this segment to see if you are guilty of some errors such as pronoun and verbal agreements.

When you start off with a singular subject, keep the pronouns and verbs that refer to the subject singular also. Mistakes in these agreements are heard on TV all the time. Nearly all the newscasters, talk show hosts, sportscasters, as well as the writers who pen the shows and commercials, misuse the plain rules. Following are sentences that are wrong! wrong! wrong!

EXAMPLES: "A person experiencing chest pains will often deny they are having a heart attack." "An employee must call if they are going to be late." "Each foodhandler must wash their hands before and after they touch food." "Watch your child around water to prevent them from drowning." "The Alsheimer's patient may become agitated when they are asked to bathe."

Okay, why is this such a problem? Because the masculine was always deferred to in the past, unless the topic specified a female subject. "A person—(he is)" "An employee—(he is)" "Each foodhandler—(his hands—he touches)" "child—(him)" "patient—(he is)"

Now we have become gender sensitive, so the idea is to blur the gender by substituting plural pronouns. Well, that is wrong and unacceptable. Fix it by using all plurals in the sentencing, "People—(they are)" "Employees—(they are)" "All foodhandlers—their hands—they touch)" "children—(them)" "patients—(they are)" Or show agreement by keeping it singular and using the words, "he or she," "him or her," and coordinating the verbs. You can use a slash, he/she, I suppose, just get those agreements right.

EXAMPLES: "A person having chest pains will often deny he or she is having a heart attack." "An employee must call if he or she is going to be late." "Each foodhandler must wash his or her hands before and after he or she touches food." "Watch your child around water to prevent him or her from drowning." "An Alsheimer's patient may become agitated when he or she is asked to bathe."

Employee manuals are noted for this type of error.

Another misuse of pronouns is switching the subjects and objects. Here are some common mistakes.

EXAMPLES:   "Me and him are going."   "Her and me will stay."   "Them are tight shoes."   "Them and us took turns."   "Me and you is friends."   "It was between he and I."   "It was handed to him and I."   "Awards were given to Kate and I."

If any of these examples look or sound right to you , you need to review the order of nominative and objective cases.  It's easy to correct these mistakes.

| NOMINATIVE | OBJECTIVE |
|---|---|
| (making or doing the action) | (receiving the action) |
| I / WE | ME / US |
| YOU / YOU | YOU / YOU |
| HE / THEY | HIM / THEM |
| SHE / WHO | HER / WHOM |
| IT | IT |

Notice the problems seem to arise when there are two or more persons or things in discussion.  It will help to leave the other person out and ask the questions, Who is doing the action?  Who is going?  "I am going."  "He is going."  It doesn't change if there are two or more.  "He and I are going."  Substitute "We" or "us" for the parties.  It might clear up the confusion because the words will sound right.  "We are going."  You wouldn't say, "Us are going," or "Him is going," or "Me is going."  Who is staying?  "We will stay," "She will stay," "I will stay."  It doesn't change.  "She and I will stay."  "They are tight shoes."  "Those are tight fitting shoes," is a better way of putting it.  "We took turns."  "They took turns."  "They took turns with us."  Are you paying attention?  "You and I are friends."  "It was between us."  "It was between him and me."  "It was handed to him and me."  "The awards were given to us, Kate and me."  It is a matter of habit.  No more bad grammar habits.

WHO VERSUS THAT: When referring to people, use "Who." "The author, who wrote this book is here." "The girl, who won the prize left today." "The man, who saved the child, was honored." Who for people, that for things or animals. "The rock, that was thrown, broke a window," "The meal, that was eaten—," "The book, that was written,— " "The dog, that barked—" etc.

YOUR and YOU'RE: Your is a possessive pronoun. "Your eyes," "Your hat," Your job," Your pen" Don't use your when you mean to use you're. You're is a contraction of you are. "You're feeling sad." "You're going to work." "You're sexy." "Your ego swells when you're flattered." Got it?

THEIR and THEY'RE: Their is also a possessive pronoun. "Their package-," "Their fault-," "Their son-" They're is a contraction of they are. "They're gone-," "They're expensive ," "They're my favorite-," "They're coming now."

ITS and IT'S: Its is a possessive pronoun. "Its flea collar.," "Its front page-," "Its glow-," "Its leaves-" Don't put an apostrophe on a possessive its. Think of its the same as his and hers. It's is a contraction of it is. "It's cold today." "It's a scary movie." "It's my turn." "It's not fair." "It's too bad." "It's going to be fun."

LAY and LIE: When you go to bed you lie down, you are going to lie down. People lie down in present or future. "Last night I lay on the couch." "I have lain there many times." People lie, lay, have/ had lain. Things are placed. "Chickens lay eggs." "You lay the book on the table." "You laid it there yesterday." "You have laid it there before." With things, it's lay, laid, have laid.

Shoulda, coulda, woulda and should of, could of, would of are all wrong. "I shoulda studied harder." "He could of been a champion." No! No! The missing word is have. You can shorten should have, could have and would have to should've, would've and could've.

Another error heard often is should have went. Please change that habit if you are guilty. Go, went, should have gone. "I should have gone to the hospital."

Be aware of tenses. Brung is not the past tense of bring. The past tense of many verbs is shown by adding ed or changing a y to an i and adding ed. (talk-talked, cry-cried) Some words change with tenses. Present tense happens now or in the future. (I eat, I will eat) "I am going to eat salad with dinner." Past tense describes actions that have taken place. "I ate fish yesterday." Past participle refers to past actions that still go on or have bearing on the present. "I have eaten at that restaurant often." The present and future perfect verb tenses (have, has, had) and the past progressive (was) must accompany past participles. "I will have eaten dinner by six." "The meal was eaten on time." Too heady? Sorry, English is a difficult language. Here is a list of some irregular verbs.

| PRESENT | PAST | PAST PARTICIPLE |
| --- | --- | --- |
| begin | began | have, has had, was begun |
| break | broke | have, has, had, was broken |
| bring | brought | have, has, had, was brought |
| buy | bought | have, has, had, was bought |
| drink | drank | have, has, had, was drunk |
| eat | ate | have, has, had, was eaten |
| fly | flew | have, has, had, was flown |

| go | went | have, has, had, was gone |
| give | gave | have, has, had, was given |
| hide | hid | have, has, had, was hidden |
| leave | left | have, has, had, was left |
| make | made | have, has, had, was made |
| ride | rode | have, has, had, was ridden |
| swear | swore | have, has, had, was sworn |
| sing | sang | have, has, had, was sung |
| speak | spoke | have, has, had, was spoken |
| write | wrote | have, has, had, was written |

Try to avoid cliché expressions such as; "Being as" or "Being as how," "You know," "You understand," Watch out for double negatives. "He don't got no money." "I don't take no bull." "I didn't see nobody there." Change to one negative. "He has no money." "I take no bull." (Maybe not as colorful, but correct never the less.) "I saw no one there." "I didn't see anyone there."

I'm not trying to give you a college degree here and there are a lot of subjects that have not been touched. Why do you need to know all this technical jargon? Well, you really don't need to know everything unless you plan to teach an English course. Plow through it anyway, you never know, you might mingle in literary circles some day and you will hold your own in discussions. You are a writer now.

Again I'll mention the annoying habit of sticking the word "at" on the ends of sentences. I don't know how or where it started, but it is pervasive. "At" does not belong on phrases such as; "Where are you?" "Where is it?" "Where do you live?" "Where can I reach you?" If you find yourself saying "at" bite your tongue.

When you hear a friend say, "I should have went," correct him. Don't let the kids get by with saying, "I seen," "We've ate," "Between you and I."

Correct them while they are young and they will thank you for it eventually.  Children learn to alter their speech from,  "Me go potty,"  "Him want horsey," to more sophisticated speech.  They can also learn proper grammar early in life.  Don't wait until they start school.  Speech patterns are pretty well set and bad habits are hard to break.  Most teachers don't catch and change grammatical errors.  Encourage children to enrich their vocabulary.  Cursing is not only an excuse for thinking, it is a substitute for poor vocabulary.

### COMMAS

I have received letters from someone who doesn't see the need for commas.  Her sentences seem to ramble on as though she does not stop to take a breath.  When you speak, you employ voice inflections and pauses to indicate separate elements and lists.  Commas in written sentences signal these inflections for the reader.  They separate clauses, phrases, items of lists, addresses, dates, words such as auxiliary verbs, adjectives and adverbs used in a series.  Commas set off quotations, interjections, parenthetical expressions and contrasting statements.

Without commas, a narrative can be confusing.

EXAMPLE:  "Before he eats Michael smokes his pipe."  "Before he eats," is a subordinate clause.  It doesn't express a complete thought, so it cannot stand alone.  "Michael smokes his pipe," is an independent clause and can function as a sentence.  The two clauses joined with a comma make sense.  "Before he eats, Michael smokes his pipe."

When you have a sentence with two independent clauses joined by coordinating conjunctions and, but, for, either—or, neither—nor, so, yet, use a comma.

EXAMPLES: "Ben likes dogs, but he is allergic to them." "Jed promised to stop drinking, yet he went on a bender." You don't use a comma before a coordinating conjunction if the following clause is dependent.

EXAMPLES: "Ben likes dogs but has allergies." "Jed promised to stop drinking yet went on a bender."

A non-restrictive phrase is one that gives incidental information in a sentence. It is set off by commas if it is not essential to the meaning of the sentence.

EXAMPLES: "The gardener, who was recommended by a neighbor, works for us on Saturdays." "My friend, who loves to dance, won the Charleston contest."

The meaning of the sentence would not be altered if the non-restrictive phrase were eliminated. A restrictive phrase does not need commas.

EXAMPLES: "The neighbor's gardener comes over here to work on Saturdays." "People who live in glass houses should not throw stones."

Commas are used after subordinate phrases to avoid confusion.

EXAMPLE: "If you want to shoot the club meets on Tuesdays." Stick a comma after the word shoot, so it makes sense. "If you want to shoot, the club meets on Tuesdays."

Commas set off introductory phrases.

EXAMPLE:     "Having   won   the   state championship, Pat decided to go for the nationals."

Commas set off contrasting statements.

EXAMPLE: "You will lose weight with diet and exercise, not by pills alone."

Use   commas   to   set   off   nouns   in   direct address.

EXAMPLE: "Madam chairman, honored guest, ladies and gentlemen, join me in song."

Use   commas   to   set   off   quotations   and   a speaker.

EXAMPLE: "Hey guys," Pete exclaimed, "let's have a party."

These are some of the uses for commas. Even if you didn't absorb the reasons for all the commas, you can see that the following sentence badly needs commas.

EXAMPLE: "Simply put messy desks which have disorganized filing reflect slovenly work habits and slothful employees counterproductive to the company."

"Simply put," is an interjection needing a comma.  Commas are needed to separate the non-restrictive modifiers, "which have disorganized filing"

and "counterproductive to the company." The
sentence becomes easier to read with commas in the
proper places. "Simply put, messy desks, which
have disorganized filing, reflect slovenly work habits
and slothful employees, counterproductive to the
company."

Is this everything you have ever wanted to
know about commas? Just get on with it and scatter
commas about, you'll do fine.

## FASHIONS AND STYLES

You don't have to set aside a chapter to write
about fashion and styles. When you describe people
in your stories, try to remember the type of clothing
they wore. Some periods of time had definite and
unique clothing styles. You may not recall exactly
what was worn, but you can give the impression of
the decade and the general mood of the people by
mentioning the wearing apparel and hairdos.

Clothing may be relevant to scenes you are
describing. How were you bundled up in the winter
when you were a kid? Did you wear leggings, muffs,
hand-knitted mittens and scarves? Did you wear
boots or galoshes? What kind of hats and coats were
worn? What were the clothes like in warm weather?
Describe the bathing suits. When you write about
school days, clarify the time sequence, and the
uniforms or trendy styles, shoes, gym wear and hair
styles. What were the dress codes? Were boys
allowed to wear jeans? Were girls allowed to wear
slacks?

Tell about the rise and fall of hemlines or
men's neckties and lapels that go from wide to
narrow and back again. Where did you fit in the
fashion picture? Were you around when men wore
stovepipe trousers, gray flannel suits, blue serge

suits or zoot suits? How about the Nehru jacket fashion or bell bottoms, plaid slacks with white belts and shoes, leisure suits, jackets with no lapels or shirts with no collars? Were the coats long, short, shapeless or tailored? Men's shoes have been hightops, wing-tips, loafers, hushpuppies, sneakers, cowboy boots, dress boots and athletic shoes. Do they make rubbers anymore?

Flesh out your images with details of the look and feel of the times. If too much description would take away from the story or if it is not necessary, skip it. But you don't want to just chronicle events as news items, you want to make them interesting. Women's styles have changed radically from bustles, long skirts, and high button shoes to the roaring twenties flapper fashions, with short, fringed dresses, bobbed hair, cloche hats and high heels. The thirties were more conservative and the forties raised hemlines again. Women started wearing brassieres and makeup. In 1947, the "New look" came in with voluminous skirts which were very cumbersome. Bobby socks, poodle skirts, crinoline petticoats, saddle shoes, reindeer sweaters were all popular during the forties and fifties. Women wore hats and gloves. Every woman wore a girdle whether she needed one or not. Remember when the mini skirts came out in the sixties? Some school officials wouldn't allow them to be worn and many businesses sent women home to "change into something respectable."

Did political persuasion influence your hair length? Men have worn their hair long, short, as crew cuts or butches, with side burns, permanents and with pony tails. How did the men in your life deal with baldness? Did they wear hair pieces? Did they grow the sides long to comb across the top? Did they just shave it all off? There were probably some odd beards, mustaches and side burns on quite a few men in your life.  If any of this has any bearing on a character sketch or anecdote, by all means include it.

Women's makeup has changed also. Remember when eyebrows were plucked out and a fine arched line was painted on?  The only lipstick color at first was bright red.  Pancake base makeup turned orange and powder was too white.  Too much rouge was garish and eye shadow was only worn for evening wear.  False eyelashes were the rage in the seventies.

A woman's hair, her "crowning glory," often reflects much of her personality by the style in which it is worn.  Before the 1920's, it was unheard of to cut women's hair.  Women were met with a great deal of opposition when they wanted to bob their long tresses to fit in with the flapper era of the twenties.  Once they got past that barrier, women have had their hair cut, dyed, bleached, curled, permed, crimped or straightened to the tune of billions of dollars.  You can reveal a lot about the women characters and yourself in your stories just by your observances of hair.  Were the coifs elegant? or au natural.  Can you picture someone with her hair pulled back severely and tucked into a bun or gathered into a snood?  As well as you can, describe bobs, beehives, flips, braids, pigtails, ponytails, Afros, dread locks, corn ribs, pompadours.  Hair may be curly, straight, permed, crimped, stiff with spray, beauty parlor regulars, or casual look, messy or neat. If you can't remember the exact style, that's okay, just give your general impression.

Then there is hair color.  Blondes may be ash blonde, strawberry, golden, platinum or dirty blonde, artificial or real.  Redheads may be auburn, carrot top, fiery, coppery, henna or real.  Browns can be chestnut, mahogany, light, dark or mousy brown. Black can be raven haired, patent leather, tinged with gray.  Gray is salt and pepper, slate, blue tinted or silvery.  White can also be silver or snowy white. All hair has texture.  Add some superlatives when describing someone's hair, such as; lustrous, shiny, thick, thin, smooth, soft, fine, wiry, coarse, wispy, limp, dry, flyaway, bushy, wavy, luxurious.  Do you see how colorful details can add to the total picture?

## SCRIPT WRITING

You may catch the drama bug and decide to offer some or all of your experiences to the film industry.  Studios and TV shows will not accept unlisted material.  You have to submit a "treatment" to an agent who might pass it on to a script writer who can transform your idea into a working script. The best way for a beginner in the business is to start with a published piece.  You might get a magazine or a newspaper to publish part of your manuscript.  Send copies to Hollywood agents.  If there is enough human interest an agent might see a potential money maker in your precious gem.  This might be a television short, a series, a documentary, a movie of the week.  It may be based on fact or a fictionalized account of an actual happening.  Your work may also find its way onto the big screen.

A treatment is a synopsis of the story accompanied by some hype to promote your efforts. You might attempt to write a script yourself.  If you want to learn how to write for TV, film or the stage, check with your library.  Some of these instruction books are very old and out of date so choose wisely. You need to list a cast of characters and extras, props, interior and exterior settings and stock shots. Stock is footage such as sunsets or airplanes taking off or landing.  Every camera angle must be numbered on both sides of the page.  Learn techniques, such as POV (point of view), which is the camera's view from the character's eyes.

When you picture the scene in your mind's eye, be aware of different movement and camera angles. Don't take away from the main focus of the scene, nevertheless, keep it interesting. If you don't have a definite camera position in mind, but you want a change, put down ANOTHER ANGLE. Location, approximate time of day, a list of characters and props must be listed before every scene. Mood, description and lighting are all helpful to the director and crew. You can put in your own directions but directors usually change everything, so don't go overboard. You don't want your script to look confusing and choppy. Make it simple and leave it to the professionals.

A teaser is a short scene to draw in the audience before the credits. This was created to keep people from switching channels before the story gets under way, so it has to be a grabber. Following is part of a teaser from an episode of a TV series, "Here Come The Brides," that my husband, Rick Tobin and I wrote. You can see a little bit of format and technique that is entailed.


"Smokey"


TEASER
FADE IN:
EXT. SEATTLE MAIN STREET - NIGHT

1. We PAN the street. The night is dark and   1.
   ominously quiet. In the heavy rolling fog,
   familiar objects appear as macabre shapes.
   A lantern swinging from a storefront gives off
   an eerie glow. The CAMERA, surveying the
   scene, is drawn to the light in Ben Perkin's

General Store.  IT moves up to the window
and peeks inside at BEN and LOTTIE sitting
at the counter surrounded by a pile of
chicken feathers and four cleaned chickens.
They are industriously plucking pinfeathers
from the last two chickens with small knives.

INT. BEN'S STORE - NIGHT

2. ANGLE ON BEN AND LOTTIE as Ben pulls  2.
out a pinfeather and inspects the chicken.
Satisfied that his task is complete, he holds
it up for Lotties's approval.

BEN
How's that?

LOTTIE
Sterling job.

Ben places the chicken on the counter and flexes his
tired fingers.

LOTTIE(CONTD)
I appreciate your help, Ben.

BEN
Well, I appreciate your company.  Days like
this, nobody comes in the store.

Lottie outwardly seems to be her usual carefree self,
but continually looks toward the door with apparent
concern.

LOTTIE
That wolf stopped howling.

BEN

Probably skirting the town looking for food.

LOTTIE
It's been a long, hard winter for the animals.

While Ben is cleaning up the mess of chicken feathers Lottie is hurrying to finish the last chicken and nicks herself with the knife.

LOTTIE (CONTD)
OW! I thought we'd be finished before dark.

BEN
It's only six o'clock.

LOTTIE
Worst fog we've ever had.  Do you think they will come in town?

BEN
Who?

3.  CLOSE ON LOTTIE.                                3.


LOTTIE
The wolves!

CUT TO
EXT. WINDOW OF BEN'S STORE - NIGHT

4. as the CAMERA becomes the eyes of a  4.
   creature peering in at them.  The CAMERA,
   moving erratically, goes around Ben's store.
   The panting sound of an animal is heard as
   it moves toward Ben's storage shack.

5.    ANGLE ON STORAGE SHACK, bolted with a    5.
heavy two by four across the door.  The two
by four is slowly lifted as we

CUT TO
INT. BEN'S STORE - NIGHT

6. Ben is tying the legs of the chickens    6.
together.  Lottie, still working on the last
chicken, nicks herself again with the knife.

LOTTIE
Darn!  I'll just cook this one pinfeathers and
all!

BEN
Here.  You're cutting yourself to ribbons.

Ben takes the chicken from her with a let me do it
smile and begins picking at it.

FADE OUT


     That's just a couple of pages to let you see
how shots and dialogue are set up.  I won't go into
the theory and technique of play writing.  That is
another book.  You may want to turn your material
into a stage play and have a local theatre company
perform it.  Little theatre groups often put on new
plays.  You can get play scripts from libraries to see
how they are constructed.  Just remember that the
stage directions in a published play were written
down by the stage manager for that particular
production.  The director did the blocking (the
placement and actions of the actors) and the stage
manager copied them down regardless of the
playwright's instructions.  Of course this has led to

friction between writers and directors because they each have their own ideas about what should happen on the stage.

In writing your autobiography, you don't always have to have a beginning, a middle and an end to your stories. People, images and recollections of events are interesting enough. When you write for film or stage you have to have a beginning, a middle and an end. Whether it's a comedy or drama you have to have a premise. You need a plot, a series of events that move and change through the course of the play. Time frames can be advanced or turned back, people can age, but you must have a common thread to your story. Put climaxes at the ends of the acts, add comedy, pathos, suspense and a great ending. Your characters must have substance. Study dialogue and make the people talk to not at one another. Write a play just for the fun of it and submit it to a local school or theatre group. You will be surprised and proud to see your work staged.

## BIBLIOGRAPHY

Most autobiographies do not have bibliographies or footnotes. You don't have to bother with them either. If you copy someone else's colorful phrase, acknowledge it when you use it. Some people pepper their books with many quotes and passages from other works. Bibliographies are lists giving the authors of books or articles and the places and dates of publications. It's a good idea to index some of your references when you use bits of quotations, poetry or news items. One reason is your readers might like to follow up on something by going to the source to read more of the information you shared. There is also the possibly that your book might be published, therefor, you will want to avoid plagiarism by giving credit where it is due.

If you feel the need to compile these lists, you can use End Notes at the end of each chapter. If you know the exact sources of your material and you want to be scientific about the whole thing, you can use footnotes.   Numbered footnotes are used to notate statistics of sources, such as, the exact pages of your reference and additional information.   The numbers should appear at the end of the quotations or facts on your pages and at the bottom in front of the source.  The index at the back of the book should alphabetically list the items and the page numbers where they appear in your work.

EXAMPLE:   In writing about tennis, Timothy Gallwey stated, "Concentration is the supreme art because no art can be achieved without it, while with it, anything can be achieved."1   The footnote at the bottom of your page would read  1 Timothy Gallwey, The Inner Game of Tennis (New York, 1974), p.90.

If you use another quote from the same book, same page number, the footnote can simply read 2 Ibid. (from the Latin word Ibidem, "in the same place")

If the book referred to is the same, but the page is different, you can put the page number in parenthesis after the passage, (p.105) or as a numbered footnote  3 Ibid.,p105.   Later on if you paraphrase something again from the same book, just write the author's last name and the page number in the footnote:  9 Gallwey, p.136.

My goodness, this is boring.  Be glad you don't have to turn your paper in to be graded.

## SELF DISCIPLINE

Writing is quite an undertaking and you must treat it as a job that has to be done. You may need discipline to stay with it. I'll try to give some helpful hints. Your work is important and interesting, keep that in mind. Remember to have note pads, pens, pencils or tape recorders handy to catch those illusive scenes flitting about in your memory. Include pertinent facts and dates so that you will be able to elaborate on them. Don't wait too long to turn your notes into story form because you might not be able to decipher them after awhile. It is not a good idea to accumulate a mountain of memos and bits of information until you finish the questions. Write as you go and watch your book take shape.

What is the best time for you to work? Some authors rise early and plunge right in. Others set a schedule and hold to it just as they would to a nine to five salaried job. You may do your best thinking at night when there are fewer distractions, although you might get too tired and sleepy to be effective. After all, this is a creative process and you want your mind clear. Set aside a time to work that will be quiet so you can concentrate. Try listening to music. Some radio stations play the "Golden Oldies." Get a headset if you will be disturbing others and listen to nostalgic tapes of your era. Music is bound to stir up fond memories and put you in the mood. When you set a time to write, make it a priority and do not procrastinate. Let people know that this is your special time, no phone calls, no interruptions. A lot can be accomplished this way because your time will not be frittered away. Eliminate some of your TV shows or tape them for later viewing. Take breaks to eat and stretch your legs and walk the dog.

If you can't write every day because of other commitments, try to fit it in two or three times a week.  You may be a weekend writer since you have to wait for your helper or you work outside the home or you need the time and space to organize your material.   If you are able to carry the questions around, where will you take notes?   Before breakfast? after coffee? in the bathroom?   What!? Some of the most creative work is done there.  Okay, riding in a car?  I said riding not driving.  Do not take notes while driving.   Waiting rooms, i.e. doctors' offices are places to make good use of your time. You are liable to wake up in the middle of the night with an idea.  Keep pen and paper on your  night stand.

This is a lesson in self discipline.  Check off the obstacles that you can overcome each day and get them out of the way.   The laundry has to be done, bills pile up, phone calls must be made, meals have to be dealt with, give these chores allotted times that will not interfere with your writing.  You have to do this or you will never find the time.  Hours turn into days, days into weeks, and so on.   Life is precious, don't waste time that could be productive. You may not have many years left.   The biggest obstacle is just getting started.   Make a list of excuses that keep you from writing.

1. You don't have the time.

2. You have to shop.

3. You are too tired.

4. You are sick or in pain.

5. You have to mind the grandkids.

6. You don't want to miss TV.

7. 8. 9. 10. The house or yard or car needs attention.

Go ahead and list all excuses, then paste them on your bathroom mirror. Make your decision to write a priority and then deal with the excuses.

If I seem to have been cajoling you to the point of becoming a pest or a bully, it's because most people are procrastinators. I know you want to do it, so you might try this. Point your finger at your image in the mirror and then point to the desk or wherever you keep your book. Watch your image as you give yourself an order to get busy. Set deadlines for certain chapters and stick to them. Share your work ethics with family and friends so they will give you encouragement and space to get it done. If you have other agendas such as, diet or exercise, you might try this method also. You see, the parts of your brain that tell you to be lazy or afraid or to have cravings, can be very convincing. You have to take charge, you are the boss. Argue with those little demons, don't let them win. Yell, scold, bribe and reward yourself, whatever it takes. If nothing else, do it because BetteLou expects you to. Yes, I do. Ask relevant questions. Be a good interviewer and please be very cooperative with yourself.

# PART II

## Self Interviewing Questions

You can open with the particulars of your childhood or you can start with a story to make an impact or maybe give a character sketch and then come back to this beginning.  Go through the questions, answer the ones that apply.  Using a first person form, write with lots of imagery and fond recollections.

Break up your narrative into chapters or sections.  You don't have to use the format that I have laid out.  You can divide your chapters into, "Early Years," Teen Years," "Twenties," "Thirties & Forties," "Fifties & Sixties," "Seventies Plus."  Or you can pick categories such as, "Background," "Careers - Marriage," "Hobbies - Crafts," "Retirement - Travel," etc.  Set up however you perceive the order of importance.  Use any of the suggestions listed with the questions.  Remember, not every question will be relevant to your experiences but I hope most will stimulate memories, germinate stories and eventuate books.

## PERTINENT FACTS

To begin, simply print your name big and bold or type it in capital letters.  Under your name print the title you have chosen.  List your vital statistics.
When and where were you born?
Name the date, time if you know it, your weight and length, the country, state, city or town, hospital, home or wherever it happened.
On this same page list your spouse(s),

significant other, children, grandchildren, great grandchildren and include if you like, whomever is close to you. Also you can list dates of births or deaths next to those names. This is similar to a genealogy chart, but a bit more personal. You can put down your profession, education, degrees, titles, religious persuasion, your age at present.

Next page; jump in with a story when you can and continue to fill out the questionnaire as best you can.

Were there any unusual circumstances connected with your birth?

How old were your parents when you were born?

What were you like as a child? Were you happy, shy, hyper, quiet, devilish, sad, sickly, robust, cute, awkward?

Describe your basic coloring and features.

From which side of the family did you get your looks?

Did your hair color change as you grew older?

What was your best feature?

Were you given a nickname based on your appearance?

Were you precocious?

Did you have self confidence?

Was there a time when self confidence saw you through a situation or a lack of it kept you out of something?

Who made you feel good about yourself?

Was there a certain relative or friend or teacher who made you feel special?

Were you a goody-goody or a holy terror?

Were you spoiled?  By whom?

Were you an active child?

What did you want to be when you grew up?

Did you set your goals early?

What was the incentive?

Did you want to be a doctor or nurse because of a hospital stay?

Did you want to be a fireman, a policeman, a movie star?

Were you going to be a teacher, a scientist, an artist or did you want to join the circus?

How differently did your plans turn out?

What were the hair styles for children when you were little?  Did girls wear pigtails or Shirley Temple curls?  Did the little boys have Buster Brown hair cuts or crew cuts?

Were your parents upset when you wanted to cut your hair or let it grow?

What were the clothes like?  Did the boys wear knickers?  Did the girls wear middies and carry muffs in the winter?

Did everyone wear hats?

Did it matter to you to be in style?

These are just some hints to get a picture of you as a child. We will get into activities and friends later.

## PARENTS

Where were your parents born?

What was their ethnic background?

Were they proud of their heritage?

How did they meet and fall in love?

Did either one speak with an accent?

Did they follow cultural customs?

If they were immigrants, was becoming American citizens very important to them?

Whatever stories your parents or relatives told about your family history should be included in your autobiography. If you grew up with different sets of parents, grandparents, guardians, adoptive parents or foster parents, write about your relationship with those grown-ups in your young life. Tell how your character was shaped by the attention given you. Did you benefit or do you consider yourself a survivor?

How much education did your parents have?

Was their education interrupted by a war or other circumstances?

What religion did your parents follow?

How important was religion in their lives?

Did it help them in times of distress?

Describe them as you remember them when you were young.

What were their personalities like?

Were they happy, funny, loud, quiet, stern, angry, sad, distant, depressed?

Do you remember them as looking healthy, strong, careworn, sickly, stout or thin, short or tall?

What was their energy level?

Think about these traits and looks and break them down into specifics so you can bring to mind images connected to them.

Who had the best sense of humor?

How was it shown?

Was the humor low key and subtle?

Was there a lot of laughter around the house?

Who inherited that sense of humor?

Did your parents tell funny stories or play practical jokes?

Did they laugh at your antics?

Did they make light of their problems so you wouldn't worry?

Was anyone embarrassed by a parent's humorous ways?

Were your parents affectionate?

Did they hug and kiss you?

Did they openly show affection to each other?

How did they display their love?

Who gave you sympathy when you were sick or injured?

Who consoled you when you encountered disappointments?

Tell about the tender moments with your parents.

Use your sense memory. Think of your mom feeding you when you were sick in bed.

Did your father shed tears as you were wheeled into surgery?

Do you remember sad farewells or sweet reunions?

Did they share grief with you?

Did they come to your aid in time of need?

Were your parents strict disciplinarians?

Were punishments harsh or unfair?

Did you fear a belt or just the threat of it?

Did your mom mete out justice or wait until dad came home?

Were you denied things or planned outings as punishments?

What were some of the escapades you got into that had you facing the consequences?

Did your parents believe in sparing the rod and spoiling the child?

Was there a problem with alcohol or drugs while you were growing up?  If so, it may be difficult to write about, but these are problems that can show up in future generations and you may be able to help with coping or avoiding the pitfalls.  Tell about embarrassment, society's attitude, the effect on the whole family.  There used to be a lack of help for domestic violence.  If this was part of your past, let it all out.  Police and even the medical profession mostly ignored the plight of families who were victims of addictive behaviors.

Who paid the bills and ran the household?

Was there neglect?

Did you suffer physical or emotional abuse?

Who was the enabling spouse?

How were anger and frustrations manifested?

How did you seek solace?

If you have been through this you must know all the terminology, codependency, relapse, recovery, self worth, etc.  You should also know that none of it was your fault.  Sometimes children of dysfunctional families become over achievers or caregivers and sometimes they sink into the abyss themselves.  If you were the one who became an alcoholic or drug addict, you have a lot to tell.  It's a big responsibility.  Write about it later, for now get on with other aspects of your past.

What did your family do in the evenings?

Did they listen to the radio?  Name some of the programs.

What was their favorite form of relaxation?

Did all of you gather around the piano to sing?

How about board games? Did you play Chess, Checkers, Monopoly, Dominoes, Canasta, Cards?

Who usually won?

Did you read or concentrate on homework?

Do you remember early TV? Did you grow up with television as your only nightly entertainment?

Who was the fixer and problem solver?

Was your father always tinkering or making something?

Did your mother sew, knit, crochet, or cook in the evenings?

If you grew up in a single parent household, that parent had to do all those things and more.

Was your house quiet or busy with activities?

What else did your parents do for entertainment?

Did they go to the movies?

Did they attend dances or concerts?

Were they big sports fans?

Were they socially active with charity or church interests?

Were you included in entertainment plans?

Were you left with baby sitters or older siblings ?

What accomplishments of your parents can you name?

This could range from an important invention to volunteer work, surviving a disaster or just quitting smoking, stopping drinking, or losing weight. Working long hours to support a family is an accomplishment.

Were they joiners?

To what clubs or organizations did they belong?

Were they gregarious?

Did they enjoy the same things?

Did one or the other join a club for business reasons?

Were they busy with political affiliations?

Were they involved in your school or scouts or sports?

Were they proud of themselves?

Was it because of a job or a talent?

Did they show pride in their heritage or ethnicity?

Were you proud of them?

Were they proud of you?

How did they show their pride?

What was your family's financial situation, low income, moderate or wealthy?

Was there a reason for the financial position, good, bad, whatever? If there was wealth, give a little background.

Was there an inheritance, a stroke of good luck, wise investments, or just plain hard work?

Did they go from rags to riches or the other way around?

Were there losses because of disasters, illnesses or maybe the stock market crash to account for bad luck?

Did your parents confide about money matters to the rest of the family?

How aware were you of monetary issues when you were young?

Did you care about status symbols?

Did you have a paper route or baby sitting jobs to help out?

When your folks couldn't afford something, did they make do?

What was shopping with your parents like?

Were they extravagant?

Did they watch every cent?

Did you enjoy tagging along to stores?

Was a shopping excursion a special treat?

Did your folks bargain or trade goods?

Do you remember shopping for a certain outfit or gift?

Did your mom buy material to make clothes?

If so, tell about homemade clothes, curtains or whatever else she sewed.

How did your parents dress?

Do you remember your dad mostly wearing business suits or dungarees?

Did your mom dress for business?

Did she wear house dresses and aprons?

Was your mom wearing slacks when you were young?

What were her dressy clothes like?

Can you picture the shoes and hats your parents wore?

Do you remember watches and pieces of jewelry?

What happened to your parents?

Did they have any memorable adventures?

Did they travel?

Were they able to enjoy retirement?

How did they spend their time?

How well did they age?

Did you have to take care of an ailing parent?

Did you understand your parents?

Did you respect them?

No fair putting down yes and no answers. Make notes before you forget and then write some stories about your parents.

## PARENTAL EMPLOYMENT

What did your father do for a living?  If he was a professional man, tell about his practice and clients.

Was he positive about his work and was he good at it?

Did he enjoy doing it or did he feel unfulfilled?

Do you remember him complaining about his job or the working conditions?

What would he rather have done with his life?

Did serving in a war alter his plans for a career?

How many employment changes did he make?

Relate some stories that he must have told concerning his work.

Did your mom work outside the home?

Was it a necessity or was it by choice?

Was it an educated career job?

Did she like working or was it drudgery?

Did mom complain about her boss?

Was she a union member?

Did you come home to an empty house?

If so, how did you feel during those years?

Did your mom take in work at home?

How did she juggle working, housework and family duties?

Did you ever visit your parents' place of employment?

Was it exciting? Why or why not?

How did you happen to go?

How often did you visit?

Did you see your parents in a different light than the home atmosphere? How did you feel?

Was it a positive or negative experience?

Did you work for or with your parents?

Were they self employed?

Did they run a small business or work a farm?

If there were perks to your parents' jobs, relate them.

Do you think working conditions have improved over the years? State your reasons.

Was anyone in your family involved in union struggles?

Explain about scabs and strike breakers.

If your parents were management, give their side as you remember it.

Did your parents have a good and fair relationship with their employees?

Did they provide decent working conditions?

How have attitudes in management changed over the years?

If the business remained in the family, how is it doing?

Have you handed down work ethics learned from your parents?

If a parent worked at a job that no longer exists, tell about it.

## SIBLINGS

Describe each of your brothers and sisters.

Give their full names and nicknames.

What are their ages in relationship to yours.

Who was the responsible one?

Who was the trouble maker?

Who was the studious one?

Who was the happy-go-lucky one?

What talents did they possess?

Where did you fit in?

Which sibling looked after the younger kids?

Tell some of the silly things you said and did together.

What little jokes did you have among yourselves?

Did you get into trouble often?

Were you interested in the same sports or hobbies?

Where did you hang out?

How did you tease one another?

Have you kept up the teasing over the years?

Who could you depend on?

How did you help each other?

Did you help with homework or sports?

What did you share?

Did you share a bedroom?

What games did you play together?

Did you share chores?

Did you fight over them?

How about clothes?

Did you wear hand-me-downs?

Did your brothers and sisters do well in school?

In what activities were they involved?

Are you supportive of each other?

How have they shown their love and concern?

What did they do with their lives?

Are they happy?

Do you phone or get together on birthdays and holidays?

Write some stories about life with your brothers and sisters during your early childhood, teen and adult years.

Does anyone interfere with the others' lives?

Was there any sibling rivalry?

If so, did you grow out of it or do you still compete?

Were there physical or mental challenges?

Do you have any regrets?

Do you wish you could take back some unkind deeds or remarks?

Name your brothers' and sisters' spouses and children. When writing about family members, be sure to give full names and explain where they fit into the family. Don't hurt anyone's feelings. Your book will be around for a long time, put lots of love into it.

## GRANDPARENTS

Where were your grandparents born?

Write the country, city of their birth and dates if you can.

Give their names and the names you called them.

Did you know them well?

Describe their personalities and tell how they influenced you. Does anyone in your family take after a grandparent in appearance, personality, traits, or quirks?

Relate some stories that relatives have told about your grandparents.

Did they spoil their grandchildren?

Were they stern, authoritative or easy going and funny?

How did they get along with the rest of the

family?

Were you close to either one?

Did your grandparents talk about life in the old country?

Did they flee from persecution or conscription?

Did a grandparent immigrate to America with a job skill?

What did your grandparents do for a living?

Were they pioneers?

How did they cope with hardships?

Did they have talents such as crocheting, needlepoint or detailed work of any kind that is becoming lost art?

What did you learn from them?

Tell as much as you can about grandparents. I will get into food and recipes later. Remember what I said about not being boring. Make these cameos interesting. "Grandpa was a blacksmith. He was a tall man with bulging muscles. I recall him standing at the forge without his shirt, the fire reflecting off the glistening sweat as he toiled."

## ANCESTORS

How far can you trace your family history?

How many family names do you know?

How many generations have been in America?

Where did they come from?

Where did they live?

What did they do?

How did they die?

What nationalities or ethnic origins combined to make up your person?

If you have any information to pass on, write it down. If you don't know too much about your family tree, who would?  This could be another chore when you have finished your book, tracing your roots.  You might have some fascinating vacations searching places and digging up facts regarding your ancestors. Create a genealogy chart as best you can and make charts for your children and grandchildren so they can have their own record.

A space to create your genealogy chart is given on the next page.

GENEALOGY CHART

## RELATIVES

Who were your aunts and uncles?   Give their complete names and how they were related to you.

Did you live near your relatives?

Were there family gatherings?

Was everyone accepted by the rest of the family?

What images do you have of them?

Did you inherit any family traits from them?

Did anyone cause problems?

Did you ever live with them?


Name your cousins.   Be specific as to where they fit in so the readers will be able to understand family connections.

Did you play with your cousins?

Were you close in age?

Have you kept in touch?

Did anyone in your family march to a different drummer?

Did you have the proverbial skeleton in the closet?

Who were the black sheep in your family history?

Were there renegades, ne'er-do-wells, horse thieves, cattle rustlers, train robbers, turncoats?

Did a bad egg turn out well?

Did anyone fall from grace?

Did someone sow some wild oats and then turn out to be a model citizen?

Did anyone become famous?  Tell about the rise to fame.

Here is where you can tell stories of heroics, adventures, dastardly deeds or comic pursuits of the people in your background.  What was the source of family pride or family shame?  Your descendants will be interested in this chapter if you have some spicy stories to relate.

## TALES AND EXPRESSIONS BY RELATIVES

Did your relatives talk about their experiences?

Who was the best story teller?

Can you remember colloquialisms that were ethnic or regional in origin?

Did they use expressions for certain acts or occasions?

What adages or sage remarks can you recall?

Try to write dialect with some of those remarks.

What was said for consolation and comfort?

What was said as warning or rebuke?

How did they give encouragement?

How was anger shown?

Did you hear maxims such as; "You can't make a silk purse out of a sow's ear," "A stitch in time saves nine," "A watched pot never boils," "Pretty is as pretty does," "A festering lily smells worse than a weed."

Have you used expressions like those when your children were growing up?

What quotes, biblical or other can you remember?

What was said when you were ill?

Did you hear, "Feed a cold, starve a fever," "Don't breathe the night air."

Were you advised to not walk under a ladder, or let a black cat cross in front of you?

What are the bedtime stories or lullabies you heard as a child?

Did you recite or sing the same ones to your children?

Were you given advise in career choices or romance?

## EARLY HOMES

Where was your earliest home?

What did it look like?

How big was your property?

If you grew up in an apartment, describe it and the building. Some of you traveled around to different countries or states, so tell about some of the memorable places where you lived.

Is there a certain amount of nostalgia connected with a home of your youth?

What was your bedroom like?

Do you remember curtains, quilts, wallpaper, pictures, toys?

What was the view from your window?

Did you slide down a banister?

Was there inside plumbing or an outhouse?

Was there a fireplace?

Did you sit on the front porch?

Where did your family gather, in the kitchen, the living room, family room, rec room?

Did you lie on the floor to  color, do homework, play games or put puzzles together?

Did your dad sit in his favorite chair and rattle his newspaper or tap his foot when you kids were too noisy?

Did your mom have a sewing room or a specific chair to sit on while she knitted, crocheted, mended or graded school papers?

Did you have a front parlor that was only used when guests came to visit?

Did you have a chesterfield sofa adorned with antimacassars?

Did you call them doilies?

Who made them?

Did you enjoy a particular section of your house?

How about playing in the attic on rainy days, going through old trunks, dressing up, finding old toys and dolls, opening up boxes and discovering treasures?

Did you roller-skate in the cellar?

Tell about your yard and playing area.

Did any part of the house frighten you when you were little?

Were you afraid to be home alone?

Describe the kitchen. Was it large and bright?

What was the stove like?

Did you have an icebox or a refrigerator?

What cooking aromas do you remember?

Do a sense memory and picture your mom preparing dinner.

Did you perch on a stool to watch her cook?

See the kitchen, touch the table and chairs.

Smell the food and spices.

Feel your mom or grandma hugging you.

Did she make the best pies?

Was the cookie jar always full?

Do you remember her pushing back a wisp of hair with the back of her hand while she was busy canning in the hot kitchen?

Did she wear aprons?

Did her hands have a faint odor of onion ?

Was the kitchen a gathering place for friends and neighbors?

Were there lively discussions around the dinner table?

Did your folks talk about the news or world affairs?

Were you grilled on what you learned in school each day?

Were you told to be quiet and eat?

What was the atmosphere at mealtimes?

What were your chores around the house?

Who emptied the ashes from the furnace or fireplace?

Who wrestled with the water pan under the ice box?

Who raked the leaves or mowed the lawn?

Who helped with the dishes and laundry?

Were you paid an allowance for doing chores?

If you lived on a farm you had a lot of chores, describe them.

Name some of the large pieces of furniture.

Did you have a breakfront, a china closet, a grandfather clock, a piano?

What kind of furniture did you have, Victorian, colonial?

Was any furniture handmade?

What are some household things that were commonplace years ago and no longer in use?

Are you familiar with butter churns, spittoons, washstands, fringed lamps, meat grinders?

Do you have some of those antiques?

Were some things thrown away that would be valued today?

How were houses cooled or heated when you were young?

What repairs were made to your house?

Who took care of things?

Who paid the bills?

Did you spend more time at a house other than your own?

Did any of your friends' houses make an impression on you?

If you grew up in an orphanage or in foster care, put it all down.

Tell about any houses in your young life, places where you lived or maybe where you spent some time. Surely you must have a story or two connected with your homes. Describe people and places and bring them to life with anecdotes.

## NEIGHBORHOODS OF YOUR YOUTH

Where did you spend most of your youth?

Was it a city, town or rural area?

Did your neighborhood have a name or a reputation?

Was there a community spirit?

Did they have block parties, clam bakes, barn dances, rummage sales, anything to bring people together?

Was the church, school or a factory or club the center of activity?

What did the neighborhood look like in the snow or rain?

Do you remember the chill of winter or the feel of spring in the air, the heat coming off the asphalt, the brilliance of the fall leaves? Think about it and write something.

Was there a special playing area?

Did you have a park nearby with tennis courts, handball courts or a golf course?

Did you play stickball on city streets?

Did you play sandlot baseball?

Did you ride a bicycle or roller-skates?

Did you ride horses?

Did you have a tree house?

Was the whole outdoors your playground with woods and fields, streams and lakes?

Did you walk to school, music and dance lessons or did you take buses, subways or cars?

Where did you buy your childhood treats?

Was there a corner candy store?

Did you run to an ice cream truck?

How much did you pay for candy or soda?

Where did you hang out as a teenager, a malt shop or a diner?

Where did you go to the movies?

How much did you pay for the tickets?

Do you remember dish nights?

Were you in a city where they had stage shows along with the films?

Did you do anything daring or dangerous growing up?

Did you play on rooftops or climb tall trees or jump out of haylofts?

Were there any hazardous playing areas?

Did you play with guns or bows and arrows?

Were there any accidents?

Did you play around railroad tracks?

Did you do things then that you would consider too dangerous now?

Who were your neighbors?

Were you on friendly terms?

Was there a local gossip?

Was there a matchmaker?

Did everyone know everybody else's business?

Did you ever have to depend on a neighbor for

help?

Was there someone special who gave comfort or advise?

Did friends and neighbors close ranks and come to the aid of those who suffered misfortunes?

Who were the heroes?

Were there gangs, murders, kidnappings?

Were there ever natural disasters where you lived?

Write about those experiences.

How did your family handle destructive storms, tornadoes, fires, earthquakes or maybe a war zone?

How did you cope?

How did you get help, food, water, medical supplies?

Did people work together?

Did some people just drift away?

Was there a mean neighbor who yelled at the kids and kept the balls that happened to roll on his or her lawn?

How did your parents handle the problem?

Was your family harassed by a psychotic neighbor?

Were you intimidated by a local bully?

Did his existence shake your self confidence?

Did you plot ways to get even?

Were you the neighborhood bully?

Are you familiar now with the area where you grew up?

Have you gone back to visit?

How has the neighborhood changed?

Is the house still there?

Are there buildings now in the fields where you used to play?

Are you ever homesick for your old stomping grounds and that way of life?

Do you live in a better neighborhood now?

## CHILDHOOD FRIENDS

Who were your buddies?

What were their nicknames?

Describe their families if they were interesting.

Did you spend time in each other's homes?

Who was your best friend?

Was the mother of your friend a good cook?

Did you ever prick your fingers and mix the blood to form a best friend pact?

What were some of the things you did together?

What made you laugh?

What were his or her good and bad traits?

Have you kept in touch?

Use your sense memory when you are recalling old friends.

Most people don't stay lifelong friends, one outgrows the other or one moves away.

How did your paths differ?

Have you ever met an old friend after many years?

Was it just like old times?

Did you still laugh at the same things?

## TOYS AND GAMES

What are your earliest memories of toys?

What do you remember playing with the most?

What materials were used in the making of your toys?

Did someone you knew create some of your playthings?

Are any of those treasures still around?

They would probably be collectors items now.

What toys made little boys happy?

Were they rocking horses, teddy bears, mechanical banks, bats, balls, guns, toy soldiers, cowboys and Indians?

What toys and dolls were popular for little girls?

What were the dolls made of, porcelain bisque, rags, rubber, plastic, corn husks, clothespins, wood, paper?

Did you give your stuffed animals and dolls names?

Did the girls play with tea sets, coloring books, sewing kits, thimbles, stoves, sinks, irons, carpet sweepers, all geared toward a future of the girls becoming homemakers?

Do you remember waking up on Christmas morning and seeing the toys under the tree?

Did you get tinker toys, Lincoln logs, erector sets, magic sets, chemistry sets, wind up toys, doll houses, bicycles, sleds, skates, big wheels, games?

Where did you keep your toys?

Did you have to keep them picked up and put away?

Were the toys of your youth more durable than the toys of today?

What parlor games did you play?

Was your family good at playing charades?

How about board games?

Did you play chess, checkers, Monopoly, Chinese checkers, Parcheesi, Backgammon, Dominoes, Scrabble, Anagrams?

Were you aware that you were being educated when you played Authors or word games?

Did you have a Ouija board?

What card games did you play, Old maid,

Michigan rummy, Pinochle, gin rummy, poker, Whisk, Uno, solitaire?

Where did you sit to play, at a game table, the kitchen table, the dining room table?

Who played with you?

When did you play these games, on rainy days or when you were snowed in?

Did you work on jig-saw puzzles, peg puzzles, Rubik's cubes?

Were those happy times for you?

Were you one of those perfectionists who could put together model ships or airplanes?

Were you artistic with drawing, painting or wood burning?

Did you learn to carve or sculpt with clay?

Did you sew, knit, crochet, needlepoint or weave?

How about collections?

Did you collect replicas of horses, dogs, owls, pigs?

Were you into things that could be profitable such as, stamps, coins or autographs?

Did someone help you make maps or Indian villages for school projects?

Did you make electrical gadgets for science fairs?

Tell about your bicycles.

Who taught you to ride?

Where were you allowed to ride?

Did you ride to school?

What outside games did you play?

Did you play hide and seek, kick the can, cowboys and Indians, king of the mountain?

Did you play house or store?

Were you good at marbles, jacks, mumblety-peg?

Did you jump rope, bounce balls, play hop scotch?

Do you have stories about skates, sleds or skis?

Do any of the young people you know play with toys and games that you played with as a youngster?

Have computers and television taken the place of games?

## HOLIDAYS

Celebrating holidays may have been some of the happiest times of your life. Sometimes they were the saddest times because of being alone or away or maybe a death in the family. Bring up memories of holidays and you will probably become very emotional. Tell about highlights of certain holidays and relate stories connected to them when you were young and through the years. Compare how you celebrated then and now.

Which holidays were special to you as a child?

Did you trade valentines in school?

Did you make fancy valentines?

Does St. Valentines day hold romantic memories for you?

What cards and gifts have you received from sweethearts and spouses?

How about the wearin' o' the green on St. Patrick's day?

Did you ever parade down Fifth Ave. in New York city?

Did you have Easter egg hunts?

Did you have your own special Easter basket and did you leave a carrot for the Easter bunny?

Did you enjoy buying new clothes and going to church on Easter Sunday?

Did you color eggs with your children?

If you celebrated Passover tell about that, the food, the family gathering.

What did you do on long memorial weekends?

Were your July fourth celebrations great with picnics and spectacular fireworks? You must have some stories there.

Labor day, another long weekend before school.

Rosh Hashanah and Yom Kippur in October.

Halloween is a favorite time for a lot of adults as well as for the children.

Did you go out on chalk night and clothesline

night before Halloween?

Did you make your costumes?

Were you given store bought candy or homemade fudge and candied apples?

Were you in Thanksgiving pageants in school?

Was there a major gathering of relatives at Thanksgiving?

Where did you meet for dinner when you were young?

Who made the best pies?

Did you help with the cooking?

Have you kept up with the traditions?

As you grew older how and where did you celebrate?

If you celebrate Hanukkah, explain what it meant to you as a child. What did you do during the eight days? Has your observance of this holiday changed over the years?

If you celebrate Christmas you may have a lot to tell.

Did you buy Christmas trees, cut your own or put up artificial trees?

Whose job was it to trim the tree?

Did everyone help or was it left up to your mom?

Did your dad struggle with a tangle of lights

Was your house all lit up on the outside?

Was the inside decorated everywhere?

Did you pick holly for the mantelpiece and mistletoe for the doorways?

Were there special handmade or personalized ornaments?

Did you have fancy stockings to hang on the fireplace?

Were milk and cookies left for Santa?

Did you have white Christmases when you were young?

Did you go caroling?

Were you in pageants at school or church?

Did you go to church on Christmas eve?

If you grew up in the Southwest, did you line your sidewalks with luminaries?

Did you usually get what you asked for?

Did you receive handmade gifts?

Did you make the rounds of friends and relatives with food and gifts?

What ethnic or national holidays do you follow?

What religious background determines the way you celebrate certain holidays?

Explain the rituals, sacred objects, decorations and food that are important. Explain the history and reasons to observe these traditions.

Did you or your children marry into a different nationality or religion?

Did this add to your culture and traditions or did it create problems?

Have you learned to celebrate new holidays because of a spouse's preferences?

Where have you spent holidays with your children and grandchildren?

Have you taken trips or cruises on holidays?

Holidays are part of your life, record them. Tell about the happy and sad events. Only you can do it. Write with love.

## CHILDHOOD ILLNESSES

Did you have any serious illnesses?

Were you quarantined for a contagious disease?

Did you have a long hospitalization?

Do you remember your first family doctor?

Was he or she nice or stern?

Did he or she make house calls?

Tell about broken bones and surgeries.

Were you given sympathy and attention when you were sick or injured?

Was it a difficult recovery?

What kept you occupied?

Who kept you company while you were recuperating?

Was it a person, a pet or maybe a stuffed animal

or doll?

What medical breakthroughs were made in your youth and how did they affect you?

Are there vaccines for most of the diseases you suffered?

What home remedies did your family use?

Did they work?

Were some based on old wives' tales or superstitions?

Do you still use any of them?

Did you have any lasting effects from an illness?

## SCHOOL DAYS

Where did you go to grammar school?

Do you remember your first day?

How did you get to school every morning?

Did you bring a lunch?

What kind of student were you?

Which teachers stick out in your memory?

Was it because they were mean or inspiring?

Did you participate in school activities?

Did your parents take you out for a treat when you graduated?

What was high school like?

Was it a much bigger school?

Do you remember the school colors, emblem or mascot?

Did you attend sporting events?

Were you on a team?

Did you get awards or letters?

Were you into academics more than sports?

Were you active in band, cheerleading, theatre?

Were you on honor roles or dean's lists?

What clubs or groups were important to you?

Did you have a high school sweetheart?

Did you go to the proms?

What kind of music was played?

Did you miss out on a lot of school events because you had to work?

Tell stories relating to chums and teachers. This was a big part of your formative years. With these stories, give an insight to your emotional growth, your popularity, your youthful hopes and dreams for the future.

Did you blossom after high school?

Did you go to college, an academy or trade school?

Did you apprentice some place?

Did you go into the service?

If you went to college, tell about fraternities and sororities.

Did you party too much?

How many times did you change your major?

Did any of your classmates become famous?

Do you keep in touch with any of them?

Did you marry one of them?

Have you attended class reunions?

Expand on this chapter. You probably have many school memories. Tell about the clothes, the hairdos, the teachers, the rules, the school grounds, the hang outs, the teams, the cliques, the lives and dreams of your fellow classmates. Get out your yearbooks and start browsing. You haven't changed too much have you?

## SPORTS

Were sports a big part of your life?

In which sports did you participate as a youngster?

Did you excel in one of them?

Did you win any championships?

Do you still have your trophies and ribbons? If you have pictures of yourself in uniforms or costumes copy them and insert them in this section.

Did you become a professional?

If so, tell about the perks, the thrills, the drawbacks.

Could you have become a professional?

Were there any circumstances that prevented you from attaining professional status such as, the war, parents, marriage, children?

Did you spend time with your children in sports?

Have you been a coach, manager, assistant or part of the cheering section?

What sports do you love as a spectator?

Do you attend sporting events?

Have you had tailgate parties?

Do you sit in front of the TV as an arm chair quarterback?

Name your favorite teams and players.

If you played a sport when you were young that is unheard of in this country or maybe one that is just no longer played, describe it. Tell about the equipment and the method of play.

Do you fish as a sport?

Do you have great fishing tales?

Where are some of the best places to fish?

What kind of fishing do you like?

Do you prefer streams, lakes or deep sea fishing?

Have you passed on your skills?

Do you hunt?

Did you hunt and fish with your father?

What kind of game have you hunted?

You can probably go on at length writing about fishing gear and guns.

Did you mount any of your kills?

If you've ever been to the Olympics, tell where and when.

Name some of the medal winners and their countries.

How have the Olympics changed?

How have big leagues changed?

What do you think of today's athletes?

What do you think of women's advances in sports?

Have you taken up any new sports?

## PETS

Pets are often an integral part of family life. Everyone has stories to tell about animals. If you didn't have a pet of your own, tell about relatives' and friends' pets. Maybe you just had a good or bad encounter with an animal. Tell your stories and describe how cute, silly, pretty, big, ferocious, intelligent, etc., the pets were from your childhood right up to the present.

What were the family dogs when you were a child?

Name the breeds. If they were mutts, describe them.

How did you acquire them?

What were their names?

Did they run free or were there leash laws then?

Were they kept outside or allowed the run of the house?

Who had the responsibility of feeding, grooming and picking up after them?

Did your dogs have eccentricities?

Did they have puppies?

Did they keep you company when you were sick?

Did you interpret the thoughts and actions of your dogs?

Were they show dogs?

Did they win trophies and ribbons?

Did they have obedience training?

Were your dogs used for hunting?

Did you have working dogs on a ranch or farm?

Were they protective?

Did they ever attack anyone?

Were they friendly, mean or shy?

Did you ever witness a dog fight?

What dogs have you had during your adult years?

If you have tales of heroics involving your dogs, now is your chance.

How about cats?

Did you have pedigreed cats?

Were they inside cats only or did they come and go as they pleased?

Did they sleep on your bed?

Did they have kittens?

Do you remember their personalities?

Did they understand your moods?

What were they fed?

How long did they live?

Did your cats attach themselves to a particular member of the family?

Did you keep exotic creatures?

Have you raised snakes, ferrets, rats, raccoons, coyotes, wolves, bears, spiders, lizards or turtles?

Are you a bird lover?

Have you had caged birds or are you a bird watcher?

Did you have tropical fish?

Do you know anyone who has a potbellied pig?

This is a fad that will probably not be popular when your great, great, great grandchildren read your book.

Have you had horses in your life?

Did you know working horses?

Were you good at horseback riding?

Do you remember stories about horses that were told to you by relatives?

If you grew up on a farm, tell about working with the livestock.

What were your chores?

What animals did you tend?

How many animals were there?

Sometimes pets are caught in the middle of divorce actions. They don't have the same sets of problems that affect children but they do become distressed by separations and change. Write about problems you have encountered in this area. You are on your own, I won't go there.

Pets mourn the death of their companions. They also grieve over the deaths of humans in their lives. They may be confused and saddened by the abrupt disappearance of a person. If they don't know there has been a death, they will wait for the return of that person, often for years. Pets do become depressed. Some pets show their grief in obvious ways and some seem to accept the loss without displaying signs of grief. Have you observed how a pet has handled the loss of a loved one?

Losing a pet is hard. People who don't care for animals just don't understand the close bonding that takes place when a pet becomes part of a family. The grief is real and long lasting. The shared love is missed very much. Some people may have been shown more attention, devotion and caring from their pets than they have from humans. As with any loss, grief takes time to heal. Writing about happy times with pets can help to preserve the fond memories. Describe the breed, size, coloring, personality and special nature of each one of your pets that meant so much to you, include pictures.

## FAMILY VACATIONS AND TRIPS

Did your family go on yearly trips when you were young?

Did you have a summer cabin?

Were the children sent to spend summers with relatives?

Did you go to Y camps, scout camps  or church camps?

Did the adults go off alone leaving the kids with sitters?

Did you go to the mountains or the beaches?

Did you bring the pets along, board them in kennels or leave them with friends?

Did you ever have a vacation romance?

Was your heart broken when it ended?

Tell about your best vacation.

What were vacations like during your early marriage years?

Did you visit in-laws?

Did anything disastrous or tragic ever happen on a vacation?

Was anyone ever lost?

What funny and exciting things happened?

How have you traveled over the years?

Did you cover the US in an RV?

Did you take cruises?

Have you been on tours to other countries?

How have your vacations changed?

Do you take it easy now, slow and relaxing instead of whirlwind trips?

Fill in pertinent facts of the time frame, place, your approximate age and some colorful details of your surroundings. You probably have albums full of photographs of vacations and trips. Make copies of your favorites and ones that relate to your stories and paste them in this chapter.

Did your family have a special place for camping?

Were you weekend campers?

What time of year did you go?

Did you hike or explore?

Did you go mountain climbing or spelunking?

Did you sing around the campfires?

Were picnics a big part of your summer fun?

Were they family outings or potluck affairs with church or club groups?

Where did they usually take place?

Did you help prepare and carry food?

Did your mom have a special dish for picnics?

Did you play games at picnics?

Did you swim or go boating?

Were there any unusual experiences?

Did you help to clean up?

Did you sing on the way home?

Have you had the same fun with your kids?

## CIRCUSES FAIRS AMUSEMENT PARKS

This is about extravaganzas you traveled to see, possibly full family excursions. Some of these may no longer be the same. Take a few moments to reminisce and describe your trips to these events when you were a child. Write also about going with a sweetheart, a spouse, or with children.

Did you go to county fairs or state fairs?

Who went along?

What did you see?

Were you ever involved with large fairs?

Did you have food, craft or livestock entries?

How about the World's fairs or Expo's?

Were you in awe of the exhibitions?

Name the year and the location.

Did you go to the Ringling Brothers' Circus in Madison Square Garden in NYC?

Did the circus set up in a big top tent in your Town?

Did you watch the animals come through from the train station?

Do you remember the side show exhibits?

What impressed you the most?

Did your parents enjoy the day?

Did you eat hot dogs and cotton candy?

Did you want to run away to the circus?

What were the carnivals like when you were young?

Did you ever win a stuffed animal?

Did you enjoy the rides?

Was it exciting being there with the bright lights, the music, the smells, the throngs of people?

Did you take your children to a circus or a World's Fair?

How did they compare with the earlier ones?

Were your children as well behaved as you were?

Do your children or grandchildren know what a geek is?

Were the kids unimpressed because they saw it all on television?

Do you still want to run away with the circus?

What entertainment parks have you been to?

Where are they?

What were some of the great rides you enjoyed as a child?

Which was your favorite park?

How much did a hot dog cost?

Did you have any funny or bad experiences at a park?

Did you go on dates to an amusement park?

Name some of those places where you spent some time when you were young.

Name some of the big name parks such as, Disneyland, Disney World, Magic Mountain, Six Flags, Sea World, Wild Animal Parks.

Did you take your children or grandchildren to any of the big parks?

Add anything of interest here. Talk about the exorbitant costs to take a family to these places.

## CARS AND OTHER TRANSPORTATION

Do you remember the cars that were driven by your parents?

Did anyone ever yell, "Get a horse"?

Give the make and the approximate year.

How did your dad take care of the family car?

Did it have a running board?

Was that car an old heap or a vintage beauty?

Do you wish you still had one of those old cars?

Who taught you to drive?

What was your first car?

How much did it cost?

What funny incidents happened with that car?

Were you a careful driver or a little wild behind the wheel?

What was your first new car?

What do you think of foreign cars?

What car do you think is the best on the market?

What do you drive now?

Which car would you like to own?

What other vehicles have you owned or driven; airplanes, motorcycles, motor scooters, dune buggies, surreys with the fringe on top?

Someone will be reading your book a hundred years from now. The transportation may not be the same as now, so describe things to the readers. Did you do a lot of traveling by buses, trains, by sea or air? Maybe some of your stories involve some sort of transportation.

## HARDSHIPS

Do you think you have benefited in any way from having gone through a difficult period?

Has it made you stronger, more aware?

Are you able to better cope with other problems?

Has a hardship made a lasting impression on you and influenced the way you deal with people?

Does the same apply to possessions or finances?

What were the particulars surrounding this

point in time? Have you analyzed your feelings?

Have you gone through therapy?

Don't be judgmental about yourself, be understanding. Your age at the time, as well as circumstances beyond your control, played a big part in your ability to cope. Some people fold from adversity and other people gain strength. If you can come to terms with your feelings, you will begin to heal some of those old wounds. Writing about them might clarify a lot of mixed emotions and thoughts. If you are carrying around guilt for your actions, it is a heavy burden. If reparations have been made, try to move on.

You may not have owned up to something that was clearly your fault. This may have led to self destructive behavior for some time. It's all right to make excuses for behavior as long as you don't use excuses for a lack of responsibility. Write about things that have been bothering you and put them into perspective. Who knows, you may want to forgive someone or bury grudges and leave the whole ordeal behind you. You have survived those evils and you are fine, write about it.

## DANGER

Do you have a story to tell about a dangerous episode in your childhood?

Remember the (who, what, when, where, why and how) for your story. Were you aware of people's reactions at the time?

Did your life change in any way because of it?

What can you tell about frightening or

dangerous happenings to members of your family?

Were there accidents or life threatening illness?

Was your spouse ever in danger?

Have you been confronted with dreaded news about your children or grandchildren?

How were lives affected by sadness or losses?

Be the story teller, your descendants will want to know the details. Some episodes are very hard to relive. When you have completed this chapter, you will feel better for having shared your sadness.

## WAR EXPERIENCES

This may be a difficult chapter for some people to write because it involves recalling traumas that are recessed in their memories. Use sense memory with caution, be sure you can deal with the emotions you uncover.

Were you a civilian victim during a war?

Which war, in what country, what years did this happen?

Can you recall the day to day existence?

How old were you and those around you?

What were some of the fears, sounds, deprivations, losses?

How did you cope?

How did it end?

What happened to the survivors?

Did you serve in the military?

What branch and in which war did you serve?

Tell about boot camp and your drill instructor.

Can you talk about some of your buddies?

Were you in combat?

Write about events over which you had no control.

Tell about wretched discomforts and boredom.

Tell about fear and panic.

What can you reveal about strategies or plans?

Write stories and images of your experiences.

Were you wounded?

How did it happen?

Tell about your treatment and recuperation.

Write about coming home and adjusting to civilian life.

If you were not in the service, write about your life during the time of war.

Was your sweetheart overseas?

Did you meet your spouse while he or she was in the military?

Did you have relatives or friends who were wounded or killed in a war?

Did you or your family contribute to the war effort?

During World War II women went to work in

defense plants and had to wear snoods to keep their long hair from getting caught in the machinery. Housewives knitted sweaters, scarves and socks for servicemen.   Cooking grease was saved for use as axle grease.   There was gas and food rationing. Children sold war bonds and stamps.   Paper and scrap metal were collected for the war effort.   Even cattails from the swamps were gathered to use for life jackets.   Men were trained to be air raid wardens. News coverage came from newspapers, magazines, radio and Newsreels in the movie theatres.   During subsequent wars the fighting action was shown on television.   The wars became personal when they were brought right into the livingrooms.   What can you tell about your life during war years?   When you finish these two chapters take a breather.

## DATING, RELATIONSHIPS AND MARRIAGE

Do you have interesting stories to tell about dating?

Did you have a steady date in high school?

What did you do and how much money did you spend?

Was this puppy love?

Was there a feeling of urgency in your high school to find a mate because chances might be slim later on?

Were there unplanned pregnancies?

Did you marry a high school sweetheart?

Did you have many romances in college?

Where did you go to meet the opposite sex?

What attracted you to a person?

Why do you think others were attracted to you?

Did physical looks take precedent in your choices?

Did you go for someone with the same interests or intellectual pursuits?

What choices have you made in looking for a mate?

Were they sometimes the wrong choices?

Did you get involved with someone because of a rebound over another person?

Were you drawn to the life of the party type who later displayed a nasty behavior change?

Were you in continual bad relationships because you chose the same controlling personalities you had experienced at home?

Did you believe you could change someone or correct bad habits?

Did it ever work?

Did you become too controlling?

Did you become an enabler for an addict?

Did you ever find the attributes that you were searching for in a mate?

Did a romance falter because of family interference?

Did it fail because you didn't live up to the expectations of your lover?

Did separations by wars or business cause a rift?

Was infidelity a factor in a breakup?

Have you learned from disappointments?

Are you attracted to people of the same sex?

Have you always known?

What are some of the problems you have encountered?

Did you make bad choices because of pressures from family or society?

Have you come to grips with what is right for you?

Have people accepted you and your lifestyle now?

Have you found happiness and fulfillment at last?

Did you find the perfect mate?

How did you and your spouse meet?

Was it love at first sight?

What attracted you to him or her?

Was yours a storybook kind of romance?

How long was your courtship?

Did you have a formal engagement?

If you have had more than one courtship and marriage, this can be a long chapter.

Were there any obstacles or setbacks?

Were there religious or ethnic differences?

What were your plans and dreams for the future?

What were your families' reactions?

Who did the proposing?

Did you elope?

Tell about the wedding preparations.

Did you have a traditional wedding with all the trappings?

Was everything perfect or did something go wrong?

Put some copies of wedding pictures, invitations, thank you notes, napkins, etc. in your book.

Who were the attendants?

What music was played during the ceremony?

What was the color scheme?

Describe the wedding dress?

What did the groom wear?

Where did the wedding take place?

Where did you hold the reception?

What was the weather like?

Where did you go on your honeymoon?

How much time were you able to take?

Was it a dream honeymoon?

Did your marriage get off to a good start?

Did you have a rocky first year?

What is his or her best feature?

What kind of laugh did your spouse have?

Give a physical description.

Tell about personality traits.

If you and your spouse are both writing your autobiographies, cross reference a lot from here on.

Give your spouse's full name, nick name, ethnic background, education, and profession. If you are widowed or divorced put it all down. Tell about coping with the problems. If you found another partner, tell about the meeting, the choices and decisions.

What were some funny things, happy times, loving and warm moments?

Relate conversations you can remember.

Tell of the struggles together, hardships, sacrifices and shared passion.

Write about your spouse's talents, skills, patience, sense of humor and idiosyncrasies if you will.

Do you feel comfortable with your mate?

Do you have the same interests?

Did you share the task of raising the children?

Have you been supportive of one another?

Were you active in community, church or

political affairs together?

If you separated, tell about the problems and causes.

What provoked anger?

Was there emotional or physical abuse?

How did you deal with it?

How was the family affected?

Was it a bitter experience?

Who had custody of the children?

How have the children adjusted over the years?

Tell about hardships the divorce caused.

Write whatever you want to about a divorce, it's your life.

Are you happy now?

## HOMES AFTER MARRIAGE

Where was your home as newlyweds?

Did you live with your parents or in-laws?

If so, was it for financial reasons or security while one of you was overseas?

How long did you live there?

Were you happy then?

Did you have parental support?

What were some of the difficulties you encountered?

Why did you move into other living quarters?

How many times have you moved?

Did you take a step up when you moved?

Did you move away from family and friends?

Explain the reasons and add some anecdotes about your early married life.

Did you start out with hand-me-downs, second-hand, or all new furniture?

Did you have to make do with whatever you had?

Did your situation get better?

What do you remember about the furnishings?

How have they changed over the years?

Were you handy around the house?

Did you ever build a house or add on rooms?

Did you buy ornaments and furniture on trips?

Have your tastes in styles changed?

Do you have some valued antiques that you can write about?

Describe them and take pictures so they will become part of your personal history.

If there are stories connected with some furniture or keepsakes, write them down.

What place do you feel is home?

Do you still consider the place where you grew up as home?

Did your houses have a lived-in comfortable look?

Were they always kept neat and tidy?

What do your children think of as home?

Describe your homes and the neighborhoods.

Did you socialize with your neighbors?

Did you rely on your neighbors for help or baby-sitting?

## YOUR CHILDREN

Give the full names and list the times, dates and places of birth of each child.

Were there any unusual details about the pregnancies or births?

Describe your children as toddlers and sprinkle pictures of them at various ages through here.

Were they given nicknames?

Tell about illnesses and injuries and how you coped.

What were their rooms, toys and games like?

Who helped with homework?

Who was the late bloomer? Which ones were shy?

Who was full of the dickens?

Were you a strict disciplinarian?

Did you spend quality time with your children?

What talents did your kids display?

Were you active in their sports or activities?

Were these casual fun interests or highly competitive?

Were you proud of their accomplishments?

What groups and organizations did they join?

Did anyone show an early interest in a profession?

Was that dream followed?

Did you have to sacrifice to send your kids through college?

Did they emulate you?

What interests or hobbies do they have now?

What sort of work do they do?

Where do they live?

How often do you see them?

When writing about your children, be kind. Get them started on their autobiographies with journals, photos and video tapes.

## PARTIES AND ENTERTAINING

What were birthday parties like when you were a child?

Were they happy affairs?

Did you have family gatherings with party hats?

Did you have a favorite flavor cake for your

birthday?

Did you have a special place for your parties?

Did you ever get a really great present that you had been yearning for?

What party games did you play, Pin the Tail on the Donkey, Bob for Apples, knocking the pinata?

You must be specific as to whom you are referring to so the reader will be able to follow your narrative.   You may be telling about Jimmy's birthday party when he was six years old.  Clarify the times and relationship so the reader   a hundred years from now will know which Jimmy you are writing about, a brother, a cousin, a son or grandson.

What parties did you have or attend as a teenager?

Did you party in college?

Did you ever have a real surprise party?

What about masquerade or theme parties?

Did you and your spouse entertain friends or business acquaintances with dinner parties?

Did you have pool or garden parties?

Did you entertain visiting relatives and friends by taking them around to see local attractions?

Have you been to crazy office parties?

Have you had anniversary or retirement parties?

You must have at one amusing story to tell

about a party.

Did you enjoy giving parties for your children?

Compare the parties and gifts of today with those of your children and yours.

Which ones were more elaborate?

Did your children appreciate the parties?

Did you appreciate the trouble your mom went through for you?

When you have finished writing this book, have a party.

## JOBS AND CAREERS

Do you remember your first job?

How much were you paid?

Was it an after school or summer job?

What did you buy with the extra cash?

What was the most enjoyable job you ever had?

What made it fun or rewarding?

What work did you dislike the most?

Was it because of the bosses, the pay, the stress, the other workers or the working conditions?

Did you find that you were sick a lot when you were unhappy or stressed out in a certain job?

Did you follow the career you trained for?

Did you study for a particular career and then

go into something entirely different?

Did your plans change because your education was cut short?

Explain the circumstances.

Do you wish you had gone into another field?

Did you trade off excitement and challenge for security?

Did you give up steady but boring work for a risky chance at something you really wanted?

Did you ever lose your shirt or go bankrupt?

Did you go through many jobs until you found the right one?

Did you make good friends at work?

Were you satisfied with your contribution?

What good or bad things can you say about job benefits?

Have you ever had to claim workman's comp from an injury?

What perks did you enjoy through jobs?

Have you had to travel with a job?

Did you have to move your family because of work?

Did you work a forty hour week or longer?

You must have many things to write regarding your employment. Tell something about what you did. Describe some of the frustrations and incompetence you encountered. What advances have been made in this field?

Do you have amusing tales to tell about your associates?

Are you retired now?

How do you fill your time?

## CLUBS, ORGANIZATIONS & VOLUNTEER WORK

Did you and your playmates have a secret clubhouse with a goofy initiation to join?

Were you a scout or a 4-H member?

Did you go to Y camps?

Were you a member of a church youth group?

You must have joined clubs in school.

Were you ever an officer?

Tell about your duties and the functions of the clubs.

Did you join clubs for business reasons.

Were you involved in a PTA?

Did you join an ethnic club?

Have you worked for a worthy cause?

Do you support charities?

Do you lend a helping hand or give financial assistance?

What are you active in now?

Have you done volunteer work?

Did you do volunteer work for a large charity

organization?

What were your duties?

Have you volunteered to work in hospitals?

Have you worked as a docent in a guild?

Did you get a sense of fulfillment or satisfaction in doing this work?

Did you help some one in need?

Was your act of kindness something you did on a personal basis?

Most volunteers work very hard at thankless jobs and get little or no recognition for their efforts. Put your approximate age and the time you devoted to the work. Give your reasons for choosing that particular charity or program. Give some information about what you did because some of those duties may become obsolete.

## TALENTS AND SKILLS

Besides your writing ability, what talents do you possess?

Did you show an early inclination towards the arts?

Were you adept at a musical instrument?

Who made you practice? If you sang, danced, performed or painted, record it all.

Were you a professional performer? If so, tell about the struggles in your career.

Did you inherit your talents?

Have you passed on your knowledge to others?

Who were your artistic idols?

In skills other than the arts, what talents do you have?

Are you an expert mechanic, a gourmet cook, cabinet maker, computer whiz?

In which particular area do you excel?

What accomplishments of yours are you most proud?

Blow your own horn and brag about your expertise.

## AWARDS AND ACKNOWLEDGMENTS

If you keep your awards and certificates in a safe place or framed on walls, leave the originals where they are and put copies in your book. Of course if you have whole rooms filled with trophies and plaques, take pictures of them and put them here. Write about each award, explain where and why you received it. Give approximate dates and your reactions to the occasion. If you have had articles written about you, put copies here.

## PERSONAL EFFECTS

This is your chapter to enter some things that you have written, published or non published. If you have written poems or songs that have been stuck in a bottom drawer somewhere, dig them out and proudly display them in your book. If you draw or paint, put in copies of your work. You might want to illustrate your book throughout with appropriate drawings. Be sure to acknowledge yourself then. If you have a category that hasn't been mentioned, put it here and write all about it.

## HOBBIES AND COLLECTIONS

Sometimes a hobby starts as a craft interest or project and becomes a very successful financial enterprise.

Did your hobby turn into a commercial venture?

Has it become a passion or just something to do in your spare time?

Has this hobby become very expensive to maintain?

Tell about your hobbies and collections while you were growing up and on into your adulthood.

Did your interests change?

What is the significance associated with your hobbies?

How did you get started?

How have you displayed your treasures?

Be sure to take lots of pictures.

Have members of your family become involved in your pastime?

Do you collect antiques?

If you made things, tell about them.

What have you learned while pursuing your hobby?

What vistas has it opened up to you?

Do you correspond with fellow enthusiasts?

Have you traveled to see or collect things?

Do you sell or trade items?

Are you a member of a fan club?

How consuming of your time has your hobby become?

Do you think of it as a relief from stress or boredom?

Have any of your collectibles become valuable?

## FOOD—MEALS AND RECIPES

What kind of food do you prefer?

Are you a meat and potatoes person?

Do you like spicy foods?

What do you consider comfort foods?

Do you eat junk food?

What ethnic or regional cuisine are you used to?

Do you want the same type of meals you had while growing up?

Have you expanded your tastes to a variety of cooking?

Are you a good cook?

Is your spouse or significant other a good cook?

Have you tried all kinds of diets?

Do you eat more healthful and nutritious foods now?

What are some favorite holiday menus?

What is your Thanksgiving dinner menu?

Who makes the best stuffing and the best pies?

Do you have wonderful recipes from your parents or grandparents?  Write them down.

What are some great recipes from your generation?

Do you have special breakfasts, lunches or dinners?

What are your favorite desserts?

Do you have restaurants or bakeries that you would like to mention?

Tell about cooking methods, canning fruits and vegetables, curing meats, pickling, smoking, drying, whatever.  Recipes will be treasured for years.  Think about food and meals and you will come up with stories of interest.  Were there any funny or disastrous meals?  Use your sense memory to conjure up family gatherings and holiday meals. Write a lot here, it will be appreciated.


## GARDENING

This may be one of the hobbies that you have written about, if so, expand on it.

Do you have a green thumb?

Did your parents have a garden?

Did you have a Victory garden?

Did you have an orchard?

Were your fruits, vegetables or flowers sold?

Did you help to harvest the crops?

Do you work hard to maintain an attractive lawn?

Tell about planting vegetables, flowers, trees, shrubbery, herbs.

What tips can you offer?

What houseplants do you have?

Were there wild flowers in the fields near the house where you grew up?

Did you pick wild blueberries and blackberries?

Did you gather pussywillows, laurel, holly or mistletoe?

## FRIENDSHIPS

Have you kept in touch with old friends through the years?

How did your paths differ?

Did you renew friendships at school reunions?

Have you and your spouse had mutual friends?

Did you meet socially with business partners?

Have you had to call upon close friends in times of need?

Who have you trusted and depended on?

Who has been your confidant?

Have you gone to the aid of a good friend?

There has got to be a story or two about friendships.

Give a couple of sheets of paper to your friends and relatives and ask them to write about you. Let them contribute to your book and maybe that will give them the incentive to start their own. You can help them with the details. Encourage your friends to relate incidents involving you. Ask them to describe your personality as they know it. Most of what they'll write will probably be flattering, if not... edit.

## LETTERS AND GIFTS

You may have saved letters that you cherished over the tears. Go through them and pick out some nice ones. If you know anyone who has saved letters from you, perhaps you can get copies. Letters can be very interesting. Include a story with each letter to set up a scenario for the correspondence.

What gifts made your eyes light up when you were young?

Was there ever a gift that you wished for but didn't think you'd get?

What handmade gifts can you remember?

Name the sweetest gift you have received.

What were some very expensive gifts given or received?

What gifts have you and your spouse exchanged?

Tell about presents given to your children.

What have they given to you and your spouse?

## HEALTH AND MEDICAL HISTORY

Give a general description of your health. Do you have any inherited health problems?

Have there been certain diseases in your family that are not supposed to be inherited but that seem to form a pattern?

If so, bring these facts to the attention of your physician.

How have you coped with medical conditions?

Here is where you can tell all about your surgeries and hospital stays.

How many times have you broken bones?

How many diseases have you had?

Are you a survivor of cancer, stroke, heart attack?

What medications are you taking now?

Tell about your spouse's health and medical history.

This is an important chapter for your descendants.

Someone may need to know of an inherited disorder.

Have you gained too much weight for your health?

Are you on a diet and exercise program?

Do you take vitamins and eat a sensible diet?

Have you changed your eating habits?

If you have to cut back on salt, sweets or fatty foods, give some tips on substitutes and recipes.

How is the health of your eyes?

How is your hearing?

Have you taken good care of your teeth?

Tell about some medical advances and procedures that have helped you. Write about some great doctors and health care workers. Write also about a misdiagnoses or malpractice and how it affected you. If you are able to start an exercise program, do it.

## GRANDCHILDREN - GREAT GRANDCHILDREN

What is the relationship like with your descendants?

Do you see them often?

Do you see yourself or your spouse in the young ones? Record what they are like now and they will be able to use your book as a reference when they start their own someday.

Tell about their energy, curiosity, interests and problems.

Who do they resemble?

Who do they take after in personality?

What talents and abilities do they possess?

What makes them laugh?

If they are very young at this point, talk about their bright futures. If they are older, write about what is going on with their lives now and where they are headed. You may not be living close enough to them to give a personal account. Write and ask questions and ask for more photos. It will be a pleasure for you and a lovely experience for family members to share memories with you. Even if you don't have stories about your grandchildren, tell about the joy and pleasure they have brought to the family. Very often divorces cause such rifts in the family structure that the grandparents are left out. You should be able to pass on good advise and wisdom and love.

## RELIGION

What religion did your parents follow?

What impressions do you remember of the religious leaders from your childhood?

What influence has religion had on your life?

Has it been a source of help to you in times of sorrow?

Were you in a church youth group?

Did you go to church socials?

Have you changed faiths?

Do your spouse and children have the same faith?

Does your religious persuasion have a bearing on your moral and ethical decisions?

Have you become more or less religious as you grow older?

What do you think of television pulpits?

Has anyone in your family joined the clergy?

Put in prayers or stories if you want.

If you are an agnostic or an atheist give your views.

## MUSIC AND ENTERTAINERS

What kind of music do you consider good listening?

Which type of music do you think of as just noise?

What were the popular songs when you were young?

What music do you like to dance to?

Do you remember camp songs, school and choir songs?

Do you and your spouse have a song that is "your song"?

Who were your favorite singers years ago?

Who do you like now?

What bands do you remember?

Name your favorite song writers, composers, musicians, conductors. If you prefer classical music, write about orchestras, concerts, operas, ballets. If you are into country western, list some of your favorites. Do you do country dancing? If you have been to stage musicals, tell about them and the stars. Name songs from musicals plays. If you like rock and roll or rap music, write about the songs, groups and performers that you think will last.

What are some of your favorite ballads?

What do you think of today's pop singers?

Compare the popular music of your day with current fads.

Did you become a professional musician?

What do you play?

How did you get stated?

With whom and where have you played?

Did you become a celebrity?

Did you have fans?

How did you handle your fame?

Have you done any other performing?

Explain your field and give hints about how to get along in show business.

Did any entertainers have a profound influence

on you?

Were you a dancer, an actor, a comedian, a magician?

Who are some of the celebrities who have worked with you?

Name some of the shows you have performed.

Who are some performers you have admired?

Did you ever meet a celebrity?

What was the occasion?

How old were you?

Were you excited?

What conversation took place?

## PSYCHIC PHENOMENA AND GHOSTS

Are you psychic?

Have you accurately predicted events that came to pass?

Have you had a bad feeling about something or someone only to have a tragic result?

Do you think you are clairvoyant?

Have you ever had feelings of deja vu?

Have you had Out of Body experiences?

Do any family members have ESP?

Do you read your horoscope in the newspaper?

Have you ever been to an astrologer?

Has an astrologer helped you make a decision that was good for you?

Did your parents or grandparents tell you ghost stories?

Was there a family ghost or a haunted house in your past?

Did aunts and uncles relate tales of the supernatural?

Did you believe them?

Have you told the same stories to your children?

Have you had any strange unexplained events that might possibly suggest the evidence of a ghost or poltergeist?

If you have been contact with a ghost, was it friendly or scary?

## ANGER

Use this chapter to pour forth your anger and frustration for injustices done to you or your family. Rant and rave if you have a grievance, here is your chance. You can express your rage about why the country is going to hell in a hand basket. Here is where you can let it all out, the little things and the big things that make you angry.

Do you keep your anger suppressed or do you burst forth and spew it all over everybody?

Are you a slow boil or can you go full tilt over dropping a pencil?

Have you harbored a resentment for something your parents did?

Was their punishment unfair?

Did you understand them better as you grew up?

Were you badly treated in a school situation?

Were you passed over for a job when you were more qualified?

Have you been fired unjustly?

Did you have disagreements with bosses or coworkers?

Were you involved in a lawsuit?

Who won and why?

Have you had bitter disputes with neighbors or companies or local governments?

How have you dealt with manipulative, domineering, self centered, overbearing people?

Have you taken heed from some critics who may have had your best interests at heart?

Have you been aware that some criticism aimed at you is arising from pure jealousy?

Have you been guilty of these personality faults?

Were you able to keep your dignity during humiliating situations?

Has your anger affected your health?

How have you vented your anger?

How have you controlled your temper?

Have you been in therapy for keeping a rage over something?

Have you been able to channel your anger into positive directions?

## SKELETONS IN THE CLOSET

This may be the chapter where you reveal some true confessions.

Did you ever do something vengeful to someone?

Do you regret your actions?

What were the circumstances?

Was it a matter of vindication?

Have you made amends?

How were other people affected?

Was this just a singular episode or a situation that went on for years?

Do you think you did wrong?

Have you gone through a guilt trip?

What has it done to you?

Were you an opportunist?

Did you step on toes and cause grief to get what you wanted?

Was this in a job situation or politics?

Did ruthlessness in business promote the

wealth you desired?

Was it accompanied by happiness?

Has a deliberate move on your part caused the demise of one or more human beings?

Did anyone in your family have a shameful past?

Was there a blemish on someone's reputation?

Did you take advantage of someone?

Was deceit involved?

Has unfaithfulness terminated a good personal relationship?

Have you been unable to make a solid commitment because of something in your past?

Are your feelings of remorse warranted?

## HAPPY TIMES

Make this a great chapter. Let the readers know you had a wonderful life. There may have been pain, sorrow, anger and hardships, but there must have been a lot of joy sprinkled throughout. Think happy.

When were you completely contented, without a care in the world?

How old were you?

Who was with you?

What exhilarating experiences have you had?

Do you get a thrill from daring and risky

adventures?

What leisure activities give you pleasure?

What is your favorite way of relaxing?

What company do you prefer to be with for a good time?

Where would you rather be right now?

Do you enjoy going out on the town?

Are you only able to relax when you are free from worry and debt?

Does peace of mind spell contentment for you?

Do you derive satisfaction from helping others?

Does surrounding yourself with aesthetic beauty make you happy?

Does a job well done make you feel elated?

Do you just like making money and gathering possessions?

List some of your happiest moments.

Was a marriage, the birth of a child, a winning lottery ticket or the safe return of a loved one among the happiest times of your life?

If you can remember some funny jokes, record them here.

Tell about the most hilarious times and things you've seen and heard and done.  Lighten up and laugh a little.

## HISTORICAL DATES AND WORLD LEADERS

Write about important or momentous events in your lifetime. You have lived through a lot of historical changes. History books might record facts from a different perspective than one who lived through them. Give your conceptions of wars, depressions, technology, civil rights, terrorist acts, hostages, space exploration.

Tell about heads of countries who have changed the world for better or worse. Name some of the men and women besides world leaders who have made a difference by their deeds and good will.

What was the first big news event that you can remember?

How old were you?

Who was the president of the United States when you were a child? Tell something about him.

What are some significant natural disasters that made headlines?

Was your family affected by floods, fires, hurricanes earthquakes, etc.?

## POLITICAL VIEWS

This can be a very revealing chapter. Be careful of using negative labels. The terminology might have quite different meanings in the future. Explain liberalism and conservatism as they pertain to the politics of today.

Why did you join the party of your choice?

Did you follow your parents' political affiliation?

Were you influenced in school?

Did you join the party for economic or ethical reasons?

Have you changed your political beliefs?

Did you ever campaign for anyone?

Were you active in local or national politics?

Who were your heroes?

Who would have become a great president?

Give your opinions of the different administrations.

Would you like to see our voting process changed?

What can you tell about assassinations and the after shocks?

What are your thoughts about local or national politicians who were booted out of office?

Do you have stories to tell of corrupt officials and graft?

Do you know about stolen money that was supposed to be used for civic projects?

Who brought shame to the office?

What positive advances have been made for your town, city and state?

What commitments were honored to promote growth and betterment of the quality of life for the citizens?

Is the nation in good hands now?

Describe the political climate.

Which political figure have you admired the most?

What can you tell about the United Nations?

Are there any political view points you would like to espouse?

## ISSUES AND LAWS

List some of the issues and laws that have affected you and your family. Some of the important issues of your day may still be of utmost concern a hundred years from now.

Have your attitudes changed over the years?

Did you ever actively protest existing laws?

Were you involved in any law making?

Have you worked in law enforcement or the court system?

How would you change the world?

This is your chance to get up on a soap box. Take a stand, give vent to your convictions. Pick any subject in which you feel strongly either way and have at it. You may not have perfect solutions to all problems but you can at least express your opinions and get a lot of gripes out of your system. Choose some of these and add your own topics to the list.
Health care, Social Security, taxes, education, military spending, government meddling, automobile safety, Civil rights, women's rights, abortions, homelessness, animal rights, gun control,

conservation, wildlife, toxic waste, air-land-sea pollution, unions, farm issues, foreign affairs, the war on drugs, drunk driving, smoking tobacco, medical research, crime prevention, victims' rights.

## PREDICTIONS, THOUGHTS AND VALUES

This can be an amusing chapter and it may prove you to be somewhat of a prophet. You can put some serious thought into some predictions about world affairs, scientific matters, your future, anything you want. Go ahead and make educated guesses. Be humorous if you like and make silly predictions, who knows, they just might come true.

Do you think countries will learn to live in peace and harmony?

Do you see a possibility of another major war?

Which countries will be involved?

Who will be our allies and who will be the enemy?

Will we make contact with aliens from other galaxies?

Do you believe we will eventually colonize the moon or Mars?

How soon do you think we will elect a woman for president?

Do you think there will be medical breakthroughs in cures for diseases such as cancer, aids, neuro-muscular, diabetes.

Do you think we will be able to clean up the environment?

Do you see a change in transportation modes?

What will housing be like in the future?

Will solar energy be in common use?

Will the work week be shortened?

What effects do you think the computer age will have on future generations?

Have you seen certain young performers that you predict will become major stars in the future?

What young sports figures will be the next champions?

How do you feel the country is heading in terms of manners, respect and morals?

Do you have any ideas about music trends, clothing or hair styles?

Make some rosy predictions for your family and friends.

Don't feel you have to come up with profound statements that will shake the world. What you have to offer is experience and first hand knowledge of events in your lifetime. You can relate your thoughts and perspectives of specific points in time. How about giving lessons on good manners. Explain the difference in attitudes and morals your generation had growing up. Tell what has made you a better human being. Perhaps your ideals and values have mellowed over the years. Maybe some concerns and interests have intensified with age. Tell what made life bearable in moments of distress. Tell about the little kindnesses that meant so much.

Tell your family how much you care about

them. Explain how certain phases will pass and that most problems will be resolved. Let family members know how important it is to get along, to keep in touch and to help one another. Pass on good wholesome values and give your blessings for the future. Go have a wonderful life.

## CONCLUSION

An idea for a paragraph or chapter will occur to you that is not covered in any of the categories. Put it down immediately, before you forget. We all have key words that will trigger the memory of a personal event. When you reminisce, keep track of what these words mean to you. Organize your thoughts, ask yourself questions, think about the subject and write it. For instance, Have you ever done anything on impulse? Was it a big mistake? Did you regret it? Did it turn out to be a terrific move? —See? Go with it, there are a lot of topics I haven't listed.

When you finish these chapters, you may be brought up to date or you may have written all that you wish to write about yourself. However, life goes on and now that you are an author you can certainly keep going. Surely, you must have confidence now. How high is your energy level? Write often, it should have become a habit by now. Start a sequel, keep a log of your travels, begin a diary. Write about your family and friends and current events.

How about writing a children's book or a romance novel, maybe a mystery? Contribute a human interest column in your local newspaper about some of your concerns or a nostalgic look at this century. Get involved in or start up an information network about a hobby or an interest of yours. Write some of those songs and poems you've been dreaming up.

While you are at it, take care of other agendas. Get those letters out to friends and relatives, exercise, clean out your closets, have a garage sale, open a business, take a trip, adopt a pet from the humane society.

Well, I have encouraged you and guided you and even badgered you to write your autobiography. I hope you have begun, if not, I shall be very disappointed in you. After all my efforts, I want some results. You can do it kiddo, make me proud of you.

# PART III

## SETTING UP

Some people only want to share their life story with their family. They don't want to share it with the world. If you want to share your life story with the world, then skip this section and go straight-away to the Afterword by publisher Jennifer DiMarco. If you'd rather your autobiography only have a few select readers, then here's how to prepare the book yourself for your family members:

## COVER

Put a neat cover on your book. You can make a collage of photographs for your cover. Select snapshots of different ages or periods of your life. You can choose a hobby or theme that best represents you, your interests and personality. Gather the photos and go to a print shop. Some of the pictures may need to be reduced in size to fit. Arrange them on good shiny card stock. Be sure to use rubberized glue for paste ups, and copy them immediately. The glue won't set or wrinkle paper and you can peel the photos off and wipe off the glue with no damage to them. Leave room for your name. This can be typeset in large print and even stamped with gold foil if you like.

You may have a title for your autobiography. Start with the title in large letters, put your name underneath and a symbol or character or photo under your name. If you want it used as a subtitle, stick your name big and bold on top, then label your subtitle and add a portrait of you below. The print shop will have some nice borders to use. Be creative, show off, make it look terrific.

## TITLE PAGE

This is a page with basically the words on the front cover. Your name and the title if you have one. That's it.

## DEDICATION

Dedicate your book to those people past or present who have special meaning in your life. You can mention as many as you like on this page.

## ACKNOWLEDGMENTS

Use this page to write about the sources of research. Mention the people who helped you with the book and praise those who put up with the fuss and mess while you were compiling and writing your book.

## PREFACE

The preface is an introduction to your book. Tell why you wrote your autobiography. Explain what prompted you to start. Write about the effort it took to gather information. Tell the obstacles you overcame and the length of time it took to finish this book.

## FOREWORD

This page is supposed to be a review of your book. Ask a close relative or good friend to give a positive review of your book and also say something about you. It will surely be flattering to your ego and why not. There should be a section in your book for this, but put a paragraph or two on this page to tantalize the readers.

## FREE PAGE

The words on this page should reflect the mood of your book. Your personality and philosophy should be represented by a meaningful phrase from you or someone else. Enter a poem or part of a poem and the author. Use a quotation from a book or an expression that you use. Keep it short and simple.

## TABLE OF CONTENTS

Name the chapters and number them starting with number one on the left side of the table. List the page they start on at the right side of the table.

# INDEX

In the back of the book is the index, listing names, places and pictures in alphabetical order and the pages where they can be found.

# BIBLIOGRAPHY

This should reference authors and publications used in your book. See Bibliography in Part I page 61.

# PART IV

## AFTERWORD

If you've come to this afterword chances are you've finished reading *Write & Publish Your Life Story: Guaranteed!* Congratulations. You're already begun your journey toward having your autobiography in print. Having a solid foundation to stand on – like the clear and concise information Ms. Tobin offers in this volume – will make writing and preparing your book for publication a straightforward and painless process.

Here at Windstorm we feel that Ms. Tobin has created a very writer-friendly guide. In keeping with that spirit, we have created a very writer-friendly approach to publishing. This is how it works:

Step 1. Purchase and read this book.

Step 2. Write your life story.

Step 3. Fill out the red form on page 165.

Step 4. Send us the form along with two copies of your story and a first class self-addressed stamped envelope. One copy of your story should be on white 8.5 x 11.0 inch paper, typed, single-sided. The other copy should be a computer file on a 3.5 inch floppy disk for PC or a 100MB Zip disk for PC. This file should be formatted to be read in Microsoft Word, Microsoft Works or Microsoft Word Pad or saved as a Rich Text Format (.rtf) file. Your book needs to be in one file only and the file name should be your last name with no hyphens, dashes or numbers (i.e. smith.doc, smith.wps or smith.rtf).

Step 5. We publish your book.

Even though Step 4 might look a little bit scary, it's not. Anyone with a computer can create one of the file types we need. If you don't have a computer, check out your local copy shop or library, or check your local phone directory under "typists" or "desktop publishing."

Let me share a little more information about the exciting Step 4. What do I mean when I say we'll publish your book? I mean we'll take your story and turn it into a book much like the one you now hold in your hands. If you send along a picture of yourself or your family, we can even put it on the front cover. We'll send you a free copy of the book when it's done and then any other copies you want you can purchase at 50% off the retail price (which will vary depending on the length of the book). We'll also sell the book to bookstores and readers around the world. For every copy of the book that sells, you'll get paid a royalty – we'll send you a check for part of the profit! You will officially be a published author.

I know this is a lot of information to take in at one time but when you send us your story we'll send you our clear, easy-to-understand contract outlining everything I've said here and more. This isn't some kind of vanity press scam – you pay nothing to have your book published and you'll never be required to buy a single copy. And don't be afraid of editors ruining your story because we won't change a single word – this is your life, after all. There are simply no hidden dangers or fine print here.

Well, there is one bit of fine print. Your book will be published in the autobiography category of our Every Life™ series. This series does have standards. Your story cannot promote or encourage hateful or illegal acts or use hateful language. If, in the judgement of our editors, your story does these things, we cannot publish it. Instead you will receive a letter stating why we can't release your book; We will return your photo and destroy all other materials.

I think that's enough reading for now. It's time to start writing! We look forward to seeing your book in print.

Sincerely,
Jennifer DiMarco
Windstorm Creative Ltd., CEO


Send your Step 4 package to:

Windstorm Creative Ltd.
Attn: Every Life, Autobiography
7419 Ebbert Dr SE
Port Orchard WA 98367

Don't forget to include your red form!
Without it, we cannot accept your package!

## Write & Publish Your Life Story
## Author Form

IMPORTANT: Every submission must be accompanied by an original form. No photocopies or reproductions of any kind are allowed. There must be one form sent per submission.

Please fill out this form completely. Print or type only. Thank you.

Your name: _____

Your phone numb_____

The title of your bo_____

_____

Your address: _____

_____

_____

_____

Where did you get your copy of this book? _____

_____

_____

_____